"Whenever you see a politician campaign with the Bible in one hand, Watch out! Because the dagger of hypocrisy will surely lie in the other."

—SENATOR WAYNE MORSE, (D-OR)

"In one hand I've a Bible
In the other I've got a gun
Well, don't you know me
I'm the man who won"

—THE EAGLES, "Outlaw Man"

"Just remember, you've never been here, you don't know me . . . Just remember, you don't know me."

—SENATOR LARRY CRAIG (R-ID)
to one of his male sexual partners

YOU DON'T KNOW ME

★ ★ ★ ★ ★

A Citizen's Guide to Republican Family Values

★ ★ ★ ★ ★

WIN McCORMACK

Illustrations by Steve Brodner

TinHouseBooks

Published by Tin House Books, Portland, Oregon, and New York, New York

Distributed to the trade by Publishers Group West, 1700 Fourth St.,
Berkeley, CA 94710, www.pgw.com

Library of Congress Cataloging-in-Publication Data

McCormack, Win.
You don't know me : a citizen's guide to Republican family values / Win
McCormack. -- 1st U.S. ed.
p. cm.
Includes bibliographical references and index.
ISBN 978-0-9794198-6-7
1. Sex scandals--United States. 2. Republican Party (U.S. : 1854-) 3.
Conservatives--United States. I. Title.
HN90.M6M43 2008
364.15'3092273--dc22   2008020384

First U.S. edition 2008

ISBN 10: 0-9794198-6-7

Interior design by Laura Shaw Design, Inc.
Cover design by Sue Walsh
Cover illustration by William Conlin

www.tinhouse.com

Printed in Canada

This book is respectfully dedicated to my Laflin forebears who involved themselves in the abolitionist struggle of the 1840s and '50s and in the founding and development of the anti-slavery Republican Party in the 1850s and '60s, and especially to my namesake, Winthrop Laflin, paper manufacturer in Lee, Massachusetts, who gave Horace Greeley three months credit on paper to launch the abolitionist *New York Tribune* (later the *New York Herald-Tribune*); Walter Norman Mills, Winthrop's nephew, who ran the Underground Railroad in Illinois; and Byron Laflin (after whom my maternal great-grandfather, Byron Laflin Smith, was named), also a nephew of Winthrop, who fought at the battle of Bull Run and served as governor of North Carolina after the Civil War. To them and the others I say, gently, Rest in Peace. If you can.

—WLM

CONTENTS

D

E

F

G

H

I

J

T

THEIR LICENSE TO DO ILL

Since the founding of the Moral Majority Coalition by Jerry Falwell in 1979, members of the American conservative movement and what has become its electoral vehicle, the Republican Party, have presented themselves as proponents of what they like to call "family values" and as leaders in the cultural wars they have unilaterally declared on liberalism and its (in their view) hedonistic, '60s-like ethos. They have railed against premarital and extramarital sex, championed the virtues of chastity and fidelity, promoted abstinence-only sex-education programs in high schools, condemned homosexuality and tried to write a prohibition against same-sex marriage into the Constitution, waged an intense and sometimes murderous struggle to outlaw abortion, and even demanded the resignation of a U.S. surgeon general because she spoke approvingly of masturbation as a safe sexual outlet for teenagers. Two of their stalwarts (Falwell and Pat Robertson) tried to blame the terrorist attacks of 9/11 on the sexual indulgences of gays and lesbians.

But in the late 1990s, there began to be signs (which escalated dramatically in number in the first decade of the new century) that all was not as it seemed in this ostensible realm of moral fervor and superiority. Republican Party officials and conservative movement spokespeople were implicated in sex scandals involving adultery, sexual abuse of underage girls, an extramarital affair with a lobbyist, sex touring abroad, sex club visitations at home and abroad, sexual harassment, spousal rape, Internet trolling for underage male sex partners, bestiality, male prostitution, instant messaging flirtation with House pages, autoerotic asphyxiation, solicitation of gay sex in an airport bathroom, and use of prostitutes, male and female.

Moral self-righteousness among the Right wing had reached such inflated proportions in the 1990s that sooner or later it had to be punctured, for, as the Good Book says, a haughty spirit goeth before a fall. But who could have imagined the depth of that fall?

When Tin House Books commissioned the in-depth research project that is reflected herein, we really had no idea of the statistics that would be unearthed. Here are some of them: 22 examples of adultery; 10 transactions with prostitutes; 3 occurrences of incest; 4 acts of indecent exposure; unwelcome advances resulting in 6 reports of sexual assault and 4 of sexual battery; 15 cases of child molestation, 13 of involvement with child pornography, 7 of soliciting sex with minors, 3 specifically concerning children 5 years old, and one concerning a 3-year-old. The grand total amounts to 110 instances of sexual misconduct by the Right, 46 of them—nearly 42 percent of the total—classifiable as pedophilia. This conduct involved 32 federally elected Republican officials or candidates for federal office, 41 state and locally elected Republican officials, 8 nationally known Republican Party figures, and 23 Republican or conservative activists.

What could possibly explain this overwhelming deviance from professed moral standards? I will explore what I see as two complementary answers to this question, one psychological and one philosophical, which mirror and reinforce each other. First I will turn to the psychological.

— — —

In his classic 1950 work, *The Authoritarian Personality*, T. W. Adorno and his team of researchers establish a link between repressed sexuality and Right-wing politics. "If the anti-democratic individual is disposed to see in the outer world impulses which are suppressed in himself," Adorno writes, "and we wish to know what these impulses are, then something may be learned by noting what attributes he most readily, but unrealistically, ascribes to the world around him . . . it seemed that the greater a subject's preoccupation with 'evil forces' in the world, as shown by his readiness to think about and to believe in the existence of such phenomena as wild erotic excesses, plots and conspiracies, and danger from natural catastrophes, the stronger would be his own unconscious urges of both sexuality and destructiveness."

Subjects of Adorno's study with strong authoritarian tendencies tended to agree with statements such as the following: "Homosexuality is a particularly rotten form of delinquency and ought to be severely punished"; "No matter how they act on the surface, men are interested in women for only one reason"; "The sexual orgies of the old Greeks and Romans are nursery school stuff compared to some of the goings-on in this country today, even in circles where people might least expect it"; and "Sex crimes, such as rape and attacks on children, deserve more than mere imprisonment; such criminals ought to be publicly whipped."

"A strong inclination to punish violators of sex mores (homosexuals, sex offenders) may be an expression of a general punitive attitude based on identification with in group authorities," Adorno comments, "but it also suggests that the subject's own sexual desires are suppressed and in danger of getting out of hand. A readiness to believe in 'sex orgies' may be an indication of a general tendency to distort reality through projection, but sexual content would hardly be projected unless the subject had impulses of this same kind that were unconscious and strongly active." Adorno and his colleagues also associate this "moralistic and punitive attitude toward the supposed sexuality of others" with a "sexual inhibition and backwardness" they found in many of their authoritarian-inclined subjects.

A study conducted by Henry E. Adams, Lester W. Wright, Jr., and Bethany A. Lohr that they describe in a 1996 issue of the *Journal of Abnormal Psychology* under the title "Is Homophobia Associated With Homosexual Arousal" might also be relevant here. The abstract of the article reads: "The authors investigated the role of homosexual arousal in exclusively heterosexual men who admitted negative affect toward homosexual individuals. Participants consisted of a group of homophobic men (n=35) . . . they were assigned to groups on the basis of their scores on the Index of Homophobia (W.W. Hudson and W.A. Ricketts, 1980). The men were exposed to sexually explicit erotic stimuli consisting of heterosexual, male homosexual, and lesbian videotapes . . . Only the homophobic men showed an increase in penile erection to male homosexual stimuli…Homophobia is apparently associated with homosexual arousal that the homophobic individual is either unaware of or denies."

Adorno describes what he calls the "pseudo-conservative." The pseudo-conservative, he writes, shows "'conventionality and authoritarian submissiveness' in his conscious thinking," but "violence, anarchic impulses, and chaotic destructiveness in the unconscious sphere…The pseudo-conservative is a man who, in the name of upholding traditional American values and institutions and defending them against more or less fictitious dangers, consciously or unconsciously aims at their abolition." In others words, the psychologically repressed authoritarians he calls pseudo-conservatives may not only be sexually problematic but may also constitute a political danger to the community.

— — —

Adorno's work (which has come in for a certain amount of methodological criticism since its publication) has recently been revised and extended by contemporary social scientists, most notably social psychologist Bob Altemeyer of the University of Manitoba. As Altemeyer explained to Watergate veteran John Dean, author of the book *Conservatives Without Conscience* (who happened upon Altemeyer's work while trying to "comprehend the personalities now dominating the conservative movement and Republican Party"), the biggest recent discovery in the field has been that there are two distinct authoritarian personalities. The first authoritarian type is the one identified by Adorno, which Altemeyer labels "right wing authoritarians" (RWAs). The second type is the authoritarian person with "social dominance orientation" (SDOs). The basic distinction is between those who follow Right-wing authoritarian movements and those who lead them.

The SDO scale measures the penchant not only for social dominance but also for economic conservatism and for a strong belief in the benefits of inequality. A personality with social dominance orientation is one "characterized by...traits of being hard, tough, ruthless, and unfeeling toward others," according to *The Oxford Handbook of Political Psychology*. Altemeyer found in his research that SDOs tend to respond in the affirmative to statements such as "Do you enjoy having the power to hurt people when they anger or disappoint you?" and "If you have power in a situation, you should use it however you have to, to get your way," and "There really is no such thing as 'right' and 'wrong'; it all boils down to what you can get away with."

However, as Dean puts it, "A striking revelation found within these studies is the fact that both right-wing authoritarians and social dominators can be accurately described as conservatives without conscience." He goes on: "It might be expected that right-wing authoritarians who are extremely religious evangelicals would have strong consciences directed by moral precepts or ethical restraints. That, however, does not appear to be the case." How to account for this seeming paradox?

Altemeyer explains that Right-wing authoritarians utilize "a number of psychological tricks and defenses that enable them to act fairly beastly," all the while believing that they are "good people." To start with, they have very little self-understanding (notice how well this fits with Adorno's finding of strong psychological repression in authoritarians). Furthermore, authoritarians have very compartmentalized minds, and so "they can just pull off a Scarlett O'Hara ("I'm not going to think about it!") whenever they want." And, they are able to "shed their guilt very efficiently when they do something wrong." Altemeyer writes in *The Authoritarian Specter*: "We end up with the irony that the people who think they are so very good end up doing so very much evil, and, more remarkably, they are probably the last people in the world who will ever realize the connection between the two."

Comments Dean: "There is no better explanation for the behavior of many Christian conservatives, for it accounts for their license to do ill, Christian beliefs notwithstanding."

Let me now turn to the philosophical side of the equation.

— — —

A modern advocate of authoritarian government whose views have had a strong impact on important segments of the American conservative movement and, through disciples of his, on the administration of George W. Bush, is Leo Strauss. Strauss rejected the idea of liberal democracy, believing in the rule of "the wise" (or, as he also called them, "philosophers") rather than the rule of the wider populace, whom he believed completely incapable of achieving wisdom. Strauss advocated that the wise use religion to control the masses, while keeping to themselves their knowledge that there is no God and therefore no given moral order (Strauss' philosophy was a unique amalgam of classical foundationalism and the anti-foundationalist existentialism of the twentieth century that descended from Nietzsche). Strauss called such sham religious posturing a "noble lie" (a phrase he took from Plato).

Strauss also rejected the liberal democratic principle that a ruler should be bound by the rule of law like the rest of the citizenry. According to Shadia Drury (in her book *Alexander Kojeve: The Roots of Postmodern Politics*), Strauss advocated what he called the "tyrannical teaching" (which he claimed Socrates espoused). Drury writes: "Strauss regards that teaching as the cornerstone of ancient wisdom. It is the view that tyranny, or rule independent of law, is the best form of government when exercised by the wise." Drury says that for Strauss, "there is no moral truth independent of the construction of power" (a thoroughly postmodern view).

Here I think we should note the resemblance between the erudite philosophical musings of Strauss on the exercise of political power and the crude underlying philosophical views that Altemeyer ferreted out in authoritarian conservatives with social dominance orientation: "If you have power in a situation, you should use it however you have to, to get your way" and "There really is no such thing as 'right' and 'wrong'; it all boils down to what you can get away with."

In his article "Ignoble Liars: Leo Strauss, George Bush, and the Philosophy of Mass Deception" (*Harper's*, June 2004), Earl Shorris writes that although most members of the Bush administration might not be followers of Strauss (or even familiar with his work), "a brief summary of Straussian doctrine suffices to demonstrate an affinity with what one might call 'the mind of the regime.'" Another thinker whose ideas seem to have an affinity with "the mind" of the Bush regime is the Nazi legal philosopher Carl Schmidt, Herman Goering's appointee as president of the Union of National Socialist Jurists. Schmidt argued the case for dictatorship over democracy on the grounds that a strong, centralized authoritarian government can better express the will of the people. And he believed that any government, to be effective—particularly in a "State of Emergency," also translated as "State of Exception"—must have at its disposal recourse to dictatorial means. Schmidt defined sovereignty thusly: "Sovereign is he who decides on the exception." It was on the basis of his theories that Hitler justified his suspension of the liberal democratic constitution of Weimar Germany.

In a July 2007 article in *Harper's*, "State of Exception: Bush's War on the Rule of Law," Scott Horton introduces the reading public to a new legal doctrine apparently current in the Bush administration and conservative legal circles: "lawfare." What is lawfare? Lawfare, according to a deputy judge advocate general of the U.S. Air Force whom Horton quotes, is "the strategy of using or misusing law as a substitute for traditional military means to achieve an operational objective." Or, as Horton quotes two neoconservative lawyers as having written, the purpose of lawfare is to "gain a moral advantage over your enemy in the court of world opinion, and potentially a legal advantage in national and international tribunals." Horton explains, "In the strange reasoning of the lawfare theorists, lawyers who defend their clients, or who present their claims to domestic or international courts, might as well be terrorists themselves. Human rights organizations that stand in court to insist that the Geneva Conventions apply to Guantánamo detainees are thus also guilty of lawfare."

Horton holds that "the lawfare doctrine is the conceptual framework that best reveals the degree to which the Bush administration has effectively declared war on the rule of law itself." The doctrine "has no antecedent in American practice, and in the end it is possible to find a precedent only if we look outside the United States to German conservative political and jurisprudential thinking between the world wars." Horton is, of course, referring primarily to the thinking of Schmidt. And couldn't Bush's reign since 9/11—with its attempts to deny the longstanding Anglo-Saxon right of habeas corpus not only to foreign prisoners at Guantánamo but also to U.S. citizens incarcerated on American soil, its assertion of the right to eavesdrop on American citizens without obtaining the court orders required by law, its official authorization of the use of recognized techniques of torture (techniques that violate not only articles of the Geneva Conventions but American law as well), and its invasion of a foreign country on a trumped-up, fear-mongering pretext—be viewed as an undeclared State of Exception (keeping in mind that this phrase can be translated as State of Emergency)? Or is it so undeclared?

In the chapter "Outlaw" from his book *Bush on the Couch*, psychoanalyst and clinical professor of psychiatry Justin A. Frank outlines what he sees as a consistent pattern of disregard for rules and law throughout Bush's life. The pattern extends in a continuum, in Frank's view, from Bush's teenage years at Andover, where he operated a business selling fake driver's licenses to fellow students, to his student days at Yale, when he was arrested by the police for disorderly conduct and detained and questioned by police in Princeton for similar conduct, to his refusal to fulfill the requirements of his military service in the Texas Air National Guard, to his arrest for drunk driving in Maine as a young adult (Frank does not mention Bush's widely rumored use of cocaine, though Bush has essentially conceded this usage by declining to deny it), to his violations of SEC reporting regulations at Harken Energy and almost certain insider trading in connection with his sales of Harken stock, to his flouting of international and domestic law as president.

Frank discerns a lifelong refusal by Bush to take responsibility for his actions and mistakes. Bush, he writes, has "comfortably and repeatedly conducted his life outside the laws of the land and the psyche." Frank believes that Bush belongs to a character type Freud called "The Exceptions." The Exception is someone who (unlike the ordinary criminal, who when breaking the law experiences an unconscious sense of guilt) feels that "normal laws don't apply to them," that they are "entitled to live outside the limitations that apply to ordinary people."

Let's now make a leap. Would it be going too far to suggest that the miscreants whose errant and sad behavior is chronicled in these pages have, ultimately, performed their misdeeds because they came to consider themselves privileged Exceptions, because they felt free to declare a personal State of Exception for themselves? That, to make use of Dean's memorable phrase, they granted to themselves a license to do ill?

— — —

Although the seminal work of Adorno and his colleagues is (despite some methodological flaws) still relevant today, there is a big difference between the context in which Adorno was operating in the late 1940s and early 1950s (and also the one in which Richard Hofstadter, author of another pathbreaking book, *The Paranoid Style in American Politics and Other Essays*, found himself a decade later) and today's. The difference is that in Adorno's time the radical Right was still only a fringe group agitating outside the mainstream of American electoral politics (in Hofstadter's era its agents were just commencing their infiltration

21

and takeover of the Republican Party), whereas in the contemporary period, the Right wing has become the establishment of the Republican Party and has used it as a vehicle to take positions of political power throughout America, from local levels on up to the presidency.

Thus, if the question Why does there seem to be a sudden epidemic of sexual misconduct by conservative Republican officials and ideologues throughout the land? is posed the immediate response is twofold: numbers and opportunity. Today there are much greater numbers of a certain kind of conservative holding positions of political power in America (there were hardly any in previous eras), and the power they wield can facilitate sexual exploitation. But, of course, this is not the whole story.

As we have seen, Adorno identified a certain personality type, which he called pseudo-conservative (there are other labels), whose violent sexual drives are (along with equally dangerous political emotions) repressed and closed to his consciousness. The pseudo-conservative projects these repressed feelings seething within him onto his political foes (as Ken Starr and the House Republicans surely did with Bill Clinton). This explains the pseudo-conservative's incessant moral hectoring of heterosexuals as well as his hostility to homosexuals (see Larry Craig). It also elucidates the obvious hypocrisy in this moral posturing, as well as the phenomenon of conservative sexual deviants legislating against their own past or future infractions (see Bob Allen and Mark Foley).

Altemeyer identified within SDOs the urge to dominate accompanied by a complete lack of moral scruples. But Altemeyer also found that both SDOs and RWAs (the type Adorno concentrated on) lack a conscience. Tellingly, and I don't think coincidentally, philosophical ideas that have permeated important segments of the American conservative movement and have had numerous adherents in the Bush administration correspond eerily to this amoral psychological makeup. Strauss, the chief progenitor of these ideas, fully embraced, according Drury, the postmodern view that "there is no moral truth independent of the construction of power." He also held (in the same vein as Schmidt) that those who hold executive power in a political system need not feel constrained by its laws. In fact, he advocated tyranny as the ideal form of government.

And so we arrive at (to employ FBI terminology) a psychological profile of the contemporary conservative Republican sexual wrongdoer: someone whose sexuality (hetero or homo) is fiercely repressed and projected onto others, but who, when his suppressed sexuality bursts forth and takes a deviant form, feels entirely justified in acting it out because he doesn't, no matter what he has been preaching, really believe in right and wrong, and who, moreover, possesses a philosophical framework (whether formalized or inchoate) that justifies that attitude. He considers himself, psychologically and philosophically, an Exception. From his perspective, he can sexually do and get away with whatever he wants. This intoxication with power may help explain the preeminence of pedophilia in our findings.

Republican abuses of political power and Republican sexual abuses in recent times are not unrelated phenomena. They have the same psychological origins and the same intellectual inspiration. They are two ugly faces of the predominant strain in contemporary American conservatism today. The crossover individual example, the political leader who has displayed both these faces to the world most dramatically, is Newt Gingrich, whose entry in our listings consumes more space than any other. The crossover collective example, in which authoritarian politics and depraved sexuality are conjoined in a single locus, is Abu Ghraib.

There might be those who would counter—in fact I think it is safe to predict that there are those who will counter—that an equivalent amount of research would disclose a similar number of sexual malefactors on the Liberal/Democratic side of the political spectrum, that this sort of behavior is not confined to Right-wing conservatives. And indeed sexual sinning is obviously not confined to any particular group of people; on the contrary it seems clearly endemic in human nature. But while you would probably find a fair amount of philandering among the population of liberal progressives, including no doubt interactions with prostitutes (in fact from long political experience I am certain of it), I don't believe you could possibly find anything approaching the same level of deviance, more often than not criminal deviance, that we have unearthed in our research, because there is not in that population the same configuration of psychological and philosophical underpinnings for it that we have identified here. To further support this belief, I return to the work of Adorno.

Adorno's group summarized its findings concerning the sexuality of right-wing authoritarian men versus non-authoritarian (I think we can read liberal) men as follows. For authoritarian men: "The hierarchical idea involved corresponds to the well-known conventional cliché and at the same time offers the high-scoring man the much needed opportunity of asserting his superiority . . . from them (women) he wants material benefits and support more than he wants pure affection, for it would be difficult for him to accept the latter. There is relatively little genuine affective involvement in his non-marital sexual relations . . . On the whole, sex is for him in the service of status, be this masculine status as achieved by pointing toward conquests, or be it social status as achieved by marrying the 'right kind' of woman."

Low-scoring (non-authoritarian) men, on the other hand, the researchers found, "tend to look primarily for companionship, friendship, and sensuality in their relations to the other sex. They are able openly to take and to give nurturance and succorance in their relations with women." It would very surprising, I think, if this kind of man assumed the role of sexual predator.

Furthermore, there is now evidence that people's political orientation is formed, or at least already manifest, quite early in life. In a study published in 2005 in the *Journal of Research in Personality* titled "Nursery school personality and political orientation two decades later," Jack Block and Jeanne H. Block, professors of psychology at the University of California, Berkeley, reported on findings concerning "the personality attributes of nursery school children who two decades later were reliably stratified along a liberal/conservative dimension." The Blocks summarize their overall findings this way: "Preschool children who 20 years later were relatively liberal were characterized as . . . self-reliant, energetic, somewhat dominating, relatively under-controlled and resilient. Preschool children subsequently relatively conservative at age 23 were described as: feeling easily victimized, easily offended, indecisive, fearful, rigid, inhibited, and relatively over-controlled and vulnerable." The nursery school boys who subsequently became conservative were "especially viewed as deviant from their peers and sensitive to being different."

According to the Blocks' long-term study, here is how the two groups compared when grown up: "At age 23, relatively Liberal young men are characterized as: introspective, life contemplative, esthetically responsive, bright, complicating of the simple, with wide interests, and relatively non-conforming. Young men scoring as relatively conservative on the LIB/CON Index proved to be independently evaluated by the various assessors as: conservative, uneasy with uncertainty, conventional and sex-typed both in their own behavior and in their social perceptions, moralistic and profferring of unasked-for advice."

Finally, the Blocks had this to say: "The (conservative) young men also display an egocentric self-image, with an orientation toward the virtues of power, a willingness to offer advice, and a concern about their status within the pecking order. This configuration of personality characteristics, although methodologically based on quite different procedures, is especially reminiscent of earlier speculations by Fromm (1941), the Berkeley studies of the authoritarian personality (Adorno et al., 1950), Rokeach (1960), and Altemeyer (1981), among others."

If you don't believe these researchers' findings (and even if you do!) look inside. What you read will astound and shock you as profoundly as it did us.

—Win McCormack

25

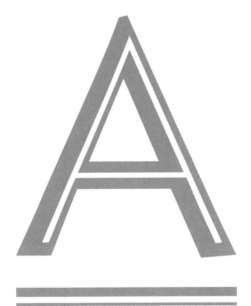

"The flames of hedonism, the flames of narcissism, the flames of self-centered morality are licking at the very foundation of our society, the family unit." [1]

—Representative BOB BARR (R-GA), speaking on the house floor in favor of the Defense of Marriage Act

ADULTERY

GEORGIA ATTORNEY GENERAL, LEADING PROPONENT OF ANTI-SODOMY LAWS, ADMITS TO AFFAIR WITH STAFFER

In June 1997, Mike Bowers, a candidate for Georgia governor and former Georgia attorney general, admitted to an affair with a subordinate in the attorney general's office. His mistress, Anne Davis, claimed the affair lasted 15 years. Bowers announced that he would resign his position as a major general in the Georgia Air National Guard because of the affair.[2]

The *Florida Times-Union* noted that, as attorney general, Bowers was "the most ardent defender of Georgia's morality laws." The paper reported that Bowers "admitted feeling hypocritical" for withdrawing a job offer in 1991 to a lesbian planning to marry another woman.[3] He claimed she engaged in illegal sexual behavior, which would undermine her ability to enforce state laws.[4]

Mistress Reveals Bowers Made Financial Payments to Her, Often By Signing Over State-Paid Expense Checks

In April 1998, Bowers' mistress Anne Davis revealed to *George* magazine that Bowers had made monthly payments of $400-$600 to her since their affair began, "often by signing over his state-paid expense checks."[5]

Bowers' wife of 35 years, Bette Rose, defended her husband's decision to financially support his mistress:

> *"When she asked Mike for help, he thought that it was the right thing to do, and I concurred. . . . I didn't think about it until it became an issue (this week). . . . I look forward to the day when Mike and I stop having to apologize for the fact that we kept our marriage together."*[6]

Bowers Refuses to Heed Fellow Republicans' Calls to Drop Out of Campaign

The *Atlanta Journal and Constitution* quoted several high-level Republican officials who suggested that Bowers should drop out of the governor's race. Bowers refused:

> *"I ran the attorney general's office in open defiance of all the damn politicians in the state. I don't owe them nothing. They can, every single one, say, 'Mike, get out,' but I'm not."*[7]

ADVOCATE OF CLINTON IMPEACHMENT ADMITS TO AFFAIR IN WHICH HE FATHERED A CHILD

In September 1998, U.S. Representative Dan Burton (R-IN) admitted to fathering a child outside of his marriage. Burton was a member of the state senate at the time of the affair and the mother of his son worked for a state agency. Burton claimed that his wife knew about his son and that he had paid child support through the years but had not seen his son until recently.[8]

Burton apologized, asserted that he had taken responsibility for his son, and insisted that the matter was "private":

> *"I have apologized to my wife and family, whom I love. I apologize to my constituents. We live in a society that rightfully depends upon people taking responsibility for their actions. I have done so in this matter."*[9]

At the time of the revelation, Burton was investigating President Clinton, whom he described as a "scumbag."[10] Burton maintained that Clinton's actions were different from his:

> *"I have never perjured myself. I have never committed obstruction of justice. I have been as straight as an arrow in my public duty. But this is private."*[11]

In 2006, Burton was presented with a True Blue Award from the Family Research Council, a Christian Right lobbying firm, for his "100% voting record on behalf of American families."[12]

REPUBLICAN CONGRESSWOMAN CRITICAL OF CLINTON ADMITS TO OWN SIX-YEAR AFFAIR WITH MARRIED MAN

In September 1998, Helen Chenoweth (R-ID) admitted to carrying on a six-year affair with Vernon Ravenscroft, a 78-year-old Republican activist from Idaho who was married. Chenoweth had been very critical of President Clinton, stating the following in her re-election campaign ads:

> *"Our founding fathers knew that political leaders' personal conduct must be held to the highest standards. President Clinton's behavior has severely damaged his ability to lead our nation, and the free world.*
>
> *"To restore honor in public office, and the trust of the American people, we must affirm that personal conduct does count, and integrity matters."*[13]

Chenoweth, who had been involved with the Family Research Council, a Christian Right lobbying firm, since 1989, claimed that God had forgiven her:

> *"I've asked for God's forgiveness, and I've received it."*[14]

Chenoweth maintained that her behavior was different than Clinton's because she was not a public figure at the time and because she did not lie about the affair. However, a reporter for the Spokane *Spokesman-Review* claimed that he had questioned her about the affair in 1995 and she responded:

> *"For heaven's sakes, that is low. That is so bizarre. I'm utterly speechless. My official answer would have to be, this indicates a measure of desperation. When they can't debate the issues,*

they turn to character assassination. . . . People who know me, know better than that. People who know Mr. Ravenscroft and his fine family know better.[15]

REPUBLICAN PRESIDENTIAL CANDIDATE, MARRIED THREE TIMES, ADMITS TO AFFAIRS; THIRD WIFE ALSO MARRIED THREE TIMES

Former New York City mayor and Republican presidential candidate Rudy Giuliani has married three times. His first marriage to Regina Peruggi, which lasted 14 years, was annulled by the Catholic Church on the grounds that the two were second cousins, once removed.[16]

Giuliani Announces Second Divorce at Press Conference Attended by Then-Girlfriend, Now Third Wife, Judith Nathan

Giuliani married television news personality Donna Hanover in 1982. The couple had two children together. At a May 2000 news conference, Giuliani announced that he planned to divorce his wife. At the time, Giuliani was seeing Judith Nathan (later to be his third wife). He introduced her to reporters at the press conference announcing his divorce. Hanover had been unaware that he planned to make the announcement and later that day held her own news conference, at which she accused Giuliani of having a long-term affair with his press secretary, Cristyne Lategano.[17]

Giuliani and Hanover settled their divorce in July 2002, reportedly for $6.8 million. According to Hanover's attorney, Giuliani was required to admit to cruel and inhumane treatment as part of the settlement because of his public affair with Nathan. In Giuliani's initial divorce petition, he accused Hanover of cruel and inhumane treatment.[18]

At a May 2000 news conference, Giuliani announced he planned to divorce Donna Hanover. This was the first Hanover had heard of it.

According to *Newsday*, Judge Judith Gische said the divorce was "so acrimonious" that she might appoint a guardian to protect the children's legal interests. In June 2001, Gische had threatened to appoint a forensic psychiatrist to examine the family.[19]

Giuliani's children have revealed that their relationship with their father is strained and have refused to campaign with him.[20]

Rumored for Years To Be Having Affair with City Hall Press Secretary

Prior to his second divorce, Giuliani repeatedly denied rumors of a long-term affair with his press secretary, Cristyne Lategano.[21]

REPUBLICAN NOMINEE FOR MINNESOTA GOVERNOR ACKNOWLEDGES AFFAIR, DENIES SWIMMING NUDE WITH TEENAGED DAUGHTER, DROPS OUT OF RACE

In October 1990, one week prior to the general election, Jon Grunseth, the Republican Minnesota gubernatorial nominee, dropped out of the race after a woman claimed that she had an affair with him while he was married to his first and second wives. Gunseth acknowledged the affair but claimed that it ended prior to his remarriage. Grunseth was also accused of swimming naked with his daughter and two other teenagers— one of whom said he tried to touch her breast—allegations that he denied.[22]

INDIANA STATE SENATOR ADMITS TO AFFAIR WITH INTERN

In September 1998, Republican Indiana State Senator Steven R. Johnson admitted to an affair with a 23-year-old intern but refused to resign:

"I have no intention of resigning. I still think I have a great deal to offer and I'm committing myself to being a great legislator."[23]

Johnson claimed that he told his wife about the affair and that the couple had been in marriage counseling.[24]

GIULIANI EMPLOYEE AND BUSH HEAD OF HOMELAND SECURITY NOMINEE PLEADS GUILTY TO ETHICS VIOLATIONS, ADMITS TO MULTIPLE AFFAIRS

In late 2006, Bernard B. Kerik, Giuliani's one-time chauffer, chief of police, and prison commissioner, and President Bush's nomination for head of Homeland Security, pled guilty to two misdemeanors for receiving $165,000 in renovations from a company accused of mob ties.[25]

In November 2007, Kerik was indicted on charges including tax fraud, obstruction of justice, and lying to the White House.[26]

Following the attacks of September 11, Kerik used an apartment that was intended for exhausted rescue workers for affairs with at least two women, including Judith Regan, the former HarperCollins publisher who worked with him on his autobiography.[27]

BILLIONAIRE CLINTON ANTAGONIST CARRIES ON AFFAIR WITH PROSTITUTE

In February 2008, *Vanity Fair* reported that Richard Mellon Scaife, the banking, oil, and aluminum heir who bankrolled the Arkansas Project—a series of investigations undertaken by the *American Spectator* that, ultimately, led to Clinton's impeachment—had carried on an affair with prostitute Tammy Vasco.[28]

Scaife's wife hired a private detective to follow her husband, and the investigator captured photographs of Scaife and Vasco in a $49 per night motel. The findings touched off a messy divorce battle that forced Scaife to pay his wife $725,000 a month in support payments.[29]

Scaife has been a reliable donor to the Republican National Convention, former Pennsylvania Senator Rick Santorum, and the conservative Western Journalism Center.[30]

CALIFORNIA CONGRESSMAN ACCUSED OF "INTENSE PERSONAL RELATIONSHIP" WITH LOBBYIST WHILE BOTH WERE MARRIED; DENIES CONFLICT OF INTEREST

In June 2000, the *Bakersfield Californian* questioned the "intensely personal relationship" between U.S. Congressman Bill Thomas (R-CA) and Deborah Steelman, a lobbyist for the prescription drug industry association. Both were married at the time.[31]

The paper suggested that the affair posed a conflict of interest because Thomas chaired the Ways and Means Committee subcommittee. The subcommittee was then drafting the Medicare prescription-drug benefit bill, which affected Steelman's employer. According to the *Bakersfield Californian*, the relationship "raises serious conflict-of-interest questions because her clients have a major stake in Thomas' work."[32]

In separate statements, Thomas and Steelman denied that a conflict of interest existed but did not deny the relationship. In an "open letter to my friends and neighbors," Thomas claimed he had "never sacrificed your interest for anything that would put me anywhere near a conflict of interest dilemma. I have never let anyone substitute their judgment on public policy for mine."[33]

Thomas also maintained that the matter was "personal":

> *"Any personal failures of commitment or responsibility to my wife, family, or friends are just that, personal."*[34]

Win McCormack **YOU DON'T KNOW ME**

Steelman called the notion that she would stoop to "an inappropriate relationship" to achieve legislative results "repugnant and sexist."[35]

WORLD BANK PRESIDENT RESIGNS POST OVER CONFLICT OF INTEREST INVOLVING ROMANTIC LIAISON WITH EMPLOYEE; FAVORITISM ALLEGED

Paul Wolfowitz, appointed president of the World Bank by President Bush in the spring of 2005, resigned from that position effective June 30, 2007 after the bank was besieged with complaints from it employees and governors relating to his relationship with Shaha Ali Reza. Wolfowitz had previously served as Under Secretary of Defense under Donald Rumsfeld.[36]

Wolfowitz, a married man with three children, reportedly had been conducting a personal relationship with Reza, a high-level employee of the World Bank, for several years. When he became president of the institution, in order to circumvent its conflict of interest rules (which prohibit relationships between bank supervisors and their employees, including indirect supervision through a chain of command), Wolfowitz arranged for Reza to receive an "external assignment" (meaning she remained on the bank's payroll) to the State Department. He also arranged for her to receive a promotion to a higher position within the bank before the start of this assignment, at an annual tax-free salary of $180,000 with an automatic annual raise of 8 percent. This salary was subsequently raised to $193, 590, at which level Reza was making more than Secretary of State Condoleezza Rice. It was this apparent favoritism toward her on Wolfowitz's part that roused the hue and cry against him within the bank.[37]

It is not clear exactly when Wolfowitz and his wife, Clare Selgin Wolfowitz, separated, but it was reportedly some time after she found out about an affair he was rumored to be having with an employee at the School of International Studies at Johns

Hopkins, where Wolfowitz had taught. Clare reportedly (she has declined to deny it) wrote to President-elect Bush (who was considering Wolfowitz for CIA Director) that this affair could pose a national security risk.[38]

Wolfowitz was one of the major advocates of launching the war in Iraq. Reza, an Arab Muslim born in Libya who is a British citizen, is said to believe very strongly in the possibility of democratizing the Middle East through force and to have had a strong influence on her lover in this regard.[39]

SEE ALSO:

Alfred Bloomingdale, Reagan Advisor (S&M)

Neil Bush, First Son/Brother (Sex Tours)

State Senator Richard Curtis (R-WA) (Prostitution)

Richard A. Dasen Sr., Conservative Activist (Rape of a Minor)

U.S. Representative Vito Fosella (R-NY) (Wedlock, Child out of)

U.S. Representative Newt Gingrich (R-GA) (Gingrich Family Values)

Mayor John Gosek (Oswego, NY) (Soliciting Sex w/ a Minor)

Rev. Ted Haggard (Prostitution)

U.S. Representative Henry Hyde (R-IL) (Impeachment, Advocate of Clinton's)

U.S. Representative Steven LaTourette (R-OH) (Lobbyist)

Dr. Laura Schlessinger, Conservative Radio Host (Nude Photos)

U.S. Representative Don Sherwood (R-PA) (Choking)

U.S. Senator David Vitter (R-LA) (Prostitution)

AFROPHOBIA

State Representative Bob Allen (R–FL) (see **Men's Rooms**)

ANNULMENT

U.S. Representative Newt Gingrich (R–GA) (see **Gingrich Family Values**)

Mayor Rudy Giuliani (New York, NY) (see **Adultery**)

ANTI-ABORTION

ANTI-ABORTION ACTIVIST ADMITS TO TERMINATING TWO PREGNANCIES

In 1990, Susan Carpenter-McMillan, an anti-abortion activist who called the emergency contraceptive drug RU-486 a "human insecticide" and organized a memorial service for 16,000 aborted fetuses, admitted to the *Los Angeles Times* that she herself had had two abortions. Carpenter-McMillan has often referred to abortion as "America's Holocaust" and remains steadfastly opposed to abortion as a legal choice, even in extreme cases of rape and incest.[40]

She terminated the first pregnancy in 1970, three years before *Roe vs. Wade* made the procedure legal. Her second abortion, in 1983, took place years after she had begun her career as a pro-life activist.[41]

When asked to explain her position and work as an activist, McMillan stated, "It was my own private life, and I don't consider myself a public figure."[42]

SEE ALSO:

U.S. Representative Bob Barr (R–GA) **(Impeachment)**

Neal Horsley, Conservative Activist **(Bestiality)**

ASPHYXIATION, AUTOEROTIC

FORMER FALWELL EMPLOYEE ACCIDENTALLY ASPHYXIATED WHILE WEARING TWO RUBBER SUITS

In June 2007, Reverend Gary M. Aldridge was found dead in his home. Aldridge had been the senior pastor at Thorington Road Baptist Church in Montgomery, Alabama, for 15 years. According to news reports, Aldridge graduated from Jerry Fallwell's Liberty University and worked for Falwell.[43]

Dr. Bob Miller, of Liberty University, noted that Aldridge was beloved by students:

> *"He went on to become one of the deans and the students loved him. He had a tremendous impact on them."*[44]

The autopsy conducted by the Montgomery, Alabama, medical examiner ruled Aldridge's death "accidental mechanical asphyxia." According to the autopsy report, when Aldridge was found he was wearing two rubberized suits and was tied in such a way that he was accidentally suffocated:

> *"The decedent is clothed in a diving wet suit, a face mask which has a single vent for breathing, a rubberized head mask having an opening for the mouth and eyes, a second rubberized suit with suspenders, rubberized male underwear, hands and feet have diving gloves and slippers. There are numerous straps and cords restraining the decedent. There is a leather belt about the midriff. There is a series of ligatures extending from the hands to the feet. The hands are bound behind the back. The feet are tied to the hands. There are nylon ligatures holding these in place with leather straps about the wrists and ankles. There are plastic cords also tied about the hands and*

The Reverend Gary Aldridge had a not very bright idea.
According to the Montgomery, Alabama, autopsy report, "The decedent
is clothed in a diving wet suit, a face mask . . . . There are
numerous straps and cords . . ."

feet with a single plastic cord extending up to the head and surrounding the lower neck. There is a dildo in the anus covered with a condom."[45]

ASSAULT, SEXUAL

COLORADO GOP ACTIVIST CONVICTED OF CHILD SEX ASSAULT, WAS A REGISTERED SEX OFFENDER

In September 2006, Randal David Ankeney was arrested for sexual assault of a child and charged with nine felonies. Ankeney was arrested while out on $100,000 bail for sexually assaulting an adult in another Colorado county. At the time, Ankeney was a registered sex offender because of a 2001 conviction of attempted sexual assault of a 13-year-old girl he had met on the Internet.[46]

Prior to his 2001 arrest, Ankeney served as a volunteer coordinator for Republican Governor Bill Owens' re-election campaign. He resigned his position as a business development representative for Owens' Office of Economic Development a day before he was arrested.[47]

EATONTON, NEW JERSEY, BOROUGH COUNCILMAN AND MUSIC TEACHER, SENTENCED TO TEN YEARS IN PRISON AFTER ADMITTING TO SEXUALLY ASSAULTING TEENAGE STUDENTS

In March 2005, Republican Eatontown Borough Councilman John J. Collins was arrested for having sex with a 16-year-old who was his former student. After his initial arrest, another woman came forward alleging that she had a sexual relationship with Collins beginning when she was 13 years old. Both girls had been affiliated with the band that Collins oversaw as a middle school music teacher but their relationships with Collins began after they had left the school.[48]

Collins resigned his seat on the Eatonton Borough Council in March 2005. He had served as a Republican councilman for 20 years. He also retired as a teacher.[49]

In August 2005, Collins was again arrested for witness tampering after he violated a court order and contacted one of the girls to attempt to get her to withhold testimony.[50]

In April 2006, Collins was sentenced to 10 years in prison for two counts of sexual assault and one count of witness tampering involving former students. Collins pleaded guilty under a deal with prosecutors. He was also required to register as a sex offender.[51]

In 2004, Collins had been named the Memorial School teacher of the year. He had been married for 37 years and had two grown sons.[52]

PENNSYLVANIA COMMITTEEMAN CHARGED WITH SEXUAL ASSAULT OF A 17-YEAR-OLD BOY

In March 2007, John Curtin, 21, was convicted of sexual assault, illegal sexual contact with a minor, and two charges of aggravated indecent assault, one with forcible compulsion.[53]

In August 2005, Curtin had hosted a party at the Stroudsburg, Pennsylvania, Days Inn, providing the minors in attendance with alcoholic beverages from the ice-filled bathtub. By 9 p.m., one 17-year-old boy had ingested 10-12 drinks, vomited in the toilet, and lain down on the bed. Later, he joined Curtin on the balcony for a cigarette. The 21-year-old Republican committeeman told the boy he wanted to talk to him and led him downstairs, through the parking lot, and around to the side of the building. It was there, the boy claimed, that Curtin grabbed him around the waist, pulled his boxers down, and tried to perform oral sex on him. The boy eventually pushed Curtin off him, and told others at the party, one of whom had witnessed the event, what had happened.[54]

Curtin's defense claimed the victim's testimony was conflicting, pointing to discrepancies in the reported time of assault, whether he was standing or sitting when it happened, whether Curtin pulled his shorts "down" or "off," and whether Curtin put "his mouth on his penis" or "his penis in his mouth."[55]

Curtin was found guilty and sentenced to six to 18 months in Monroe County Correctional Facility followed by a year's probation. County Judge Jerome Cheslock stayed the sentence pending a yearlong appeal process.[56]

CONNECTICUT MAYOR ARRESTED FOR SEXUALLY ABUSING TWO YOUNG GIRLS, USED PROSTITUTE TO ARRANGE ENCOUNTERS

In 2001, then-Waterbury, Connecticut, Mayor Philip Giordano was arrested for sexually abusing two young girls when they were eight and ten years old. The girls were the daughter and the niece of a prostitute with whom Giordano was also sexually involved. The FBI learned of the crimes during an undercover investigation of corruption in the Giordano administration. In 2003, a federal jury convicted Giordano of violating the girls' civil rights and a judge sentenced him to 37 years in prison. In 2007, Giordano pleaded no contest to state sexual-assault charges relating to his crimes against the two girls and was sentenced to 18 years in prison to run concurrently with his federal sentence.[57]

Giordano ran against Democratic Senator Joe Lieberman in 2000.[58]

Sued City for Back-Pay While in Prison

In August 2007, Giordano filed a lawsuit against the City of Waterbury for back vacation and sick pay. Giordano claimed he would split the money between his parents and his victims.[59]

Sought Job in Bush Administration with Department of Education

During the trial, the prosecutor revealed that Giordano had sought a job with the U.S. Department of Education during President George W. Bush's presidency. In a letter to a lobbyist who was helping him get the job, Giordano said that Bush had brought "respect back to the White House."[60]

SEE ALSO:

Councilman Keola Childs (Kealakekua, HI) (Child Molestation)

Carey Lee Cramer, Republican Media Consultant (Child Molestation)

"Republicans have old-fashioned extramarital affairs with other adults. Those really are moral lapses that are private and more easily forgiven and very different from taking advantage of a young person who works for you when you're president."[61]

—BILL KRISTOL, Conservative Commentator and Co-Founder of Project for the New American Century

BAD SEX WRITING

WIFE OF VICE PRESIDENT CHENEY PENS RACY NOVEL WITH LESBIAN LOVE SCENES

During the 2004 re-election campaign of George W. Bush and Dick Cheney, a leading New York paperback publisher cancelled plans to reissue a racy novel that Cheney's wife, Lynne, had originally penned in 1981, after the conservative scholar complained that the book didn't represent her "best work."

"If there is a serious demand for this 25-year-old book, I am confident that America's used bookstores will be able to satisfy it," said Cheney's attorney.[62]

Some critics mocked *Sisters*, whose lesbian scenes seemed to fly in the face of the Bush administration's support for a constitutional amendment banning gay marriage:

> *"The women who embraced in the wagon were Adam and Eve crossing a dark cathedral stage—no, Eve and Eve, loving one another as they would not be able to once they ate of the fruit and knew themselves as they truly were. She felt curiously moved, curiously envious. . . . she saw that the women in the cart had a passionate, loving intimacy forever closed to her. . . . Let us go away together, away from the anger and imperatives of men. . . . And then we shall go to bed, our bed, my dearest girl."* [62a]

TEXAS COMPTROLLER AND ABSTINENCE CHAMPION WRITES "PORNOGRAPHIC" NOVEL

In 2006, after serving as a state legislator and as U.S. Senator Kay Bailey Hutchison's state director, Susan Combs was elected comptroller of public accounts. Though the Associated Press called her "a darling of Texas conservatives" and noted her advocacy of abstinence education, in 1990 Combs penned *A Perfect Match*, a romance novel featuring a number of steamy sex scenes criticized as "trashy" and "pornographic" by her Democratic opponent.

"Everybody thinks it's fun," countered Combs. "It's light-hearted and entertaining."[63]

VICE PRESIDENT CHENEY'S CHIEF OF STAFF PENNED NOVEL FEATURING BESTIALITY AND YOUNG PROSTITUTES

In his 2001 novel, *The Apprentice*, former Cheney Chief of Staff I. Lewis "Scooter" Libby graphically describes sex scenes between a young prostitute and animals:

> *"At age ten the madam put the child in a cage with a bear trained to couple with young girls so the girls would be frigid and not fall in love with their patrons. They fed her through the bars and aroused the bear with a stick when it seemed to lose interest."*[64]

> *"There were odd tales of her sexual prowess, and they said she had coupled with dogs and men and several of the boys at once."*[65]

CONSERVATIVE TALK SHOW HOST WROTE AN ARRAY OF LEWD SCENES IN HIS 1999 NOVEL

Bill O'Reilly's 1999 crime novel, *Those Who Trespass*, dubbed "flimsy, tin-eared," and "super-steamy," by *Entertainment Weekly*, contains a number of graphic sex scenes. One begins with

"At age ten the madam put the child in a cage with a bear trained to couple with young girls so the girls would be frigid and not fall in love with their patrons."
—*from* The Apprentice, *a novel by I. Lewis Libby*

Shannon Michaels, a GNN News Correspondent, and Ashley Van Buren, a tenacious tabloid reporter, playing a game that Shannon devised, in which they take turns ordering each other to remove an article of clothing or touch themselves in an erotic fashion—he was down to his underwear and she could see "movement there."[66]

Shannon uses his turn to ask Ashley to cup and lift her breasts, an act by which he could tell she was getting "extremely" aroused. At this point, he figures it's safe to quit the game and dive headfirst between her legs, "licking the areas around her most erogenous zone . . . within seconds, his tongue was inside her, moving rapidly."[67]

O'Reilly doesn't forget to remind readers time and time again how pleasurable this is for her; she climaxes twice before even heading up to his king-size bed. Upstairs, he continues to bring her into the throws of ecstasy, and before long, of course, she shudders to another climax, thinking how much she needed "this release."[68]

Shannon then kneels behind Ashley:

"It felt so good that Ashley thought she would lose control. He was speaking in hushed tones, telling her how much he enjoyed her body, using words that in polite conversation would have been vulgar, but in this context were extremely erotic. His hands firmly gripped her buttocks."[69]

After four orgasms, Ashley falls flat on her stomach and "silently marvel[s] at Shannon's stamina."[70]

The epilogue features a final scene—strangely reminiscent of O'Reilly's conversations with Andrea Mackris—that takes place in the shower of Tommy O'Malley's Caribbean hotel room: "Ashley felt two large hands wrap themselves around her breasts and hot breath on the back of her neck. . . . Tommy O'Malley was naked and at attention."[71]

BATTERY, SEXUAL

TRINITY BAPTIST CHURCH PASTOR AND VALUES CRUSADER ARRESTED FOR SEXUAL BATTERY OF CHILDREN

In May 2006, Robert Gray, the pastor of Trinity Baptist Church, was arrested on capital sexual-battery charges. One accuser charged that he kissed her inappropriately when she was a third-grader at Trinity Christian Academy. A male student came forward to say that the pastor had fondled him when he was only nine or ten years old. In the end, more than 20 separate allegations were lodged against Gray.[72]

Gray gained notoriety when he was photographed in *Life* magazine, castigating Elvis Presley for corrupting America's youth. Under his leadership, Trinity hosted such anti-gay activists as Anita Bryant.

Gray died while awaiting trial.[73]

ANTI-ABORTION ACTIVIST CLAIMS BELIEFS CAME FROM TIME SPENT IN JAIL ON RAPE CONVICTION

In March 2005, the ten-year-old son of Howard Scott Heldreth was arrested after he tried to take a glass of water to Terri Shiavo. Heldreth and his wife are members of Operation Save America, a group that actively protests against abortion and homosexuality. When his son was arrested, Heldreth said that his religious beliefs developed while he was in prison in Ohio in 1992 and 1993. Heldreth refused to give specifics of why he was in prison, but the *Charlotte Observer* reported that he was convicted of sexual battery and that the incident involved a young woman at a college party.[74]

In 1999, Heldreth was charged with assault after threatening a doctor at an Illinois abortion clinic.[75]

OHIO GOP COUNTY COMMISSIONER SENTENCED TO EIGHT YEARS IN PRISON FOR SEXUAL BATTERY OF TWO UNDERAGE GIRLS

In January 2004, David Swartz was arrested for sexual battery of a minor. Swartz had been a Republican Richland, Ohio, county commissioner since 1996. He resigned after his arrest.[76]

A second girl came forward, and additional charges were added to his indictment. In February 2004, Swartz entered a guilty plea and admitted:

"I engaged in oral sex with a minor."[77]

In April 2004, Swartz was sentenced to eight years in prison after he pleaded guilty to two felony counts of sexual battery, two counts of felony gross sexual imposition, and one misdemeanor intimidation count. Swartz was accused of sexual conduct with two girls that began when one girl was six years old and the other 11 years old.[78]

SEE ALSO:

Mark A. Grethen, GOP Activist and Donor **(Republican of the Year)**

BESTIALITY

RADICAL ANTI-ABORTION ACTIVIST ADMITS TO SEX WITH ANIMALS AND MEN BEFORE FINDING JESUS AFTER SERVING JAIL TIME FOR DRUG DEALING

In 2005, Neal Horsley, the anti-abortion activist behind the Nuremberg Files—a Web site advocating the murder of abortion doctors and imprisoning homosexuals—told Alan Colmes that he had sex with animals while growing up on a farm:

"Absolutely. I was a fool. When you grow up on a farm in Georgia, your first girlfriend is a mule."[79]

When he returned to Colmes' show, he hinted at using inanimate objects for his sexual gratification:

"If we had a warm watermelon out in the field, I might give it a name."[80]

Six years earlier, Horsley made similar confessions in an *Esquire* profile, including admitting that, despite the JAIL FAGGOTS bumper stickers he sold on his Web site, he engaged in sexual activity with men:

"When I was young, anything that gave me penile friction I'd engage in. Men, mules, I'd fuck anything."[81]

The profile noted that Horsley had a religious conversion after serving time in jail for drug dealing. After he converted, Horsley devoted himself to social conservatism. His Web site at the time of the article contained graphic pictures of homosexual sex and bestiality and contained identifying information about abortion providers. Some of these providers had been attacked and killed, putting Horsely's Web site into the spotlight.[82]

*"When you grow up on a farm in Georgia,
your first girlfriend is a mule."*
—Neil Horsely

Admits to Pressuring Ex-Girlfriend to Terminate Her Pregnancy

Esquire's profile on the anti-abortion activist featured his admission that when a onetime girlfriend had become pregnant, he had begged her to have an abortion. When she refused, he chose never to see his unwanted child.[83]

SEE ALSO:

I. Lewis "Scooter" Libby, Vice President Dick Cheney's Chief of Staff (**Bad Sex Writing**)

Supreme Court Justice Clarence Thomas (**Harassment, Sexual**)

BLOW JOBS

U.S. Representative Newt Gingrich (R-GA) (see **Gingrich Family Values**)

Glenn Murphy, Jr., President of the Young Republican National Federation (see **Unwanted Sex Acts**)

County Commissioner David Swartz (Richland, OH) (see **Battery, Sexual**)

Stephen White, Conservative Activist (see **Soliciting Sex w/ a Minor**)

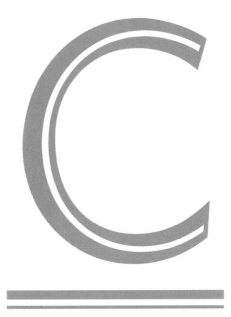

"I think that the mother killing the two children in South Carolina vividly reminds every American how sick the society is getting and how much we need to change things . . . The only way you get change is to vote Republican."[84]

—Representative NEWT GINGRICH (R–GA), referring to child killer Susan Smith

CHAT ROOM

SPOKANE MAYOR CAUGHT SEEKING TO DATE, OFFERING INTERNSHIP TO INVESTIGATOR POSING AS 18-YEAR-OLD BOY; ADMITTED TO HOMOSEXUAL RELATIONS

In May 2005, Spokane, Washington, Mayor Jim West admitted to surfing gay Internet chat rooms and to offering gifts to a young man he met online, including a City Hall internship, but denied allegations that he molested young boys. The *Spokesman-Review* published the story and hired a computer expert to pose as the 18-year-old West met on the Internet. The paper claimed that two convicted felons who had spent time 20 years earlier with West when they were Boy Scouts alleged the molestation.[85]

West denied the molestation allegations:

> *"I didn't abuse them. I don't know these people. I didn't abuse anybody, and I didn't have sex with anybody under 18—ever—woman or man."*[86]

But West did not deny having had homosexual relations:

> *"Allegations about my private life were twofold. I categorically deny allegations about incidents that supposedly occurred 24 years ago as alleged by two convicted felons and about which I have no knowledge. The newspaper also reported that I have visited a gay chat line on the Internet and had relations with adult men. I don't deny that."*[87]

West apologized for his actions in a written statement:

> *"I want to sincerely apologize to you personally for the shame I have brought to the Mayor's office and the city. I stumbled and let you down."*[88]

West was voted out of office in a recall election in December 2005. He died of cancer in July 2006.[89]

In Online Chat Calls Self "Very Closeted"

According to transcripts of the online chats, West called himself "closeted" and said he did not like the gay agenda:

> *"Remember, I'm very closeted. No one knows I like guys. Except the few guys I've been with and highly trusted. It's just that the openly gay guys are a little over the top for me. I don't really like the in-your-face attitude some guys have. And the massive political agenda either. I say live and let live. Most gay guys turn me off, too."*[90]

In Political Career, Maintained Strong Anti-Gay Bias

According to the *Seattle Post-Intelligencer*, West opposed gay rights and advocated for conservative measures against gays during his political career:

> *In more than 20 years in the Legislature, West had initiated legislation to outlaw sexual contact between consenting teenagers; supported a bill that would have barred gays and lesbians from working for schools, day care centers and some state agencies; voted to define marriage as a union between a man and a woman; and, as Senate majority leader, allowed a bill that would ban discrimination against gays and lesbians to die in committee without a hearing.*[91]

CHILD MOLESTATION

LONGTIME TOWN CLERK AND COUNTY COMMISSIONER ACCUSED OF ASSAULTING TEENAGED BOY AT STATE REPUBLICAN CONVENTION

In November 1998, Boothbay Harbor, Maine, Town Clerk and Lincoln County Commissioner Merrill Robert Barter pleaded not guilty to molesting a teenage boy during the state Republican convention. Barter had served as town clerk since 1953 and was on the county commission for 28 years.[92]

According to the grand jury's indictment, Barter "did intentionally subject [the male victim] to a sexual contact, the [victim] not having expressly, impliedly acquiesced in the sexual contact."[93]

OREGON CHRISTIAN COALITION LEADER ACCUSED OF MOLESTING FAMILY MEMBERS, NO CHARGES FILED DUE TO STATUTE OF LIMITATIONS

In August 2006, the Gresham, Oregon, police reported that Lou Beres, leader of the Oregon Christian Coalition, had admitted in interviews to molesting preteen female family members but that charges could not be filed because of statute of limitations. Along with his Christian Coalition position, Beres was also active in the Republican party and had served as a delegate to the prior two national Republican conventions.[94]

The police reported that Beres said he had received counseling through his church that corrected his behavior.[95]

The allegations first surfaced in November 2005. At the time, Beres denied the charges and blamed "personal and political enemies."[96]

In March 2006, one of Beres' victims sued him in Multnomah County Circuit Court for $2.1 million, alleging that Beres molested her from 1963 to 1966.[97]

LEGISLATIVE AIDE TO REPUBLICAN CONGRESSMAN PLEADS NO CONTEST TO CHARGE OF MOLESTING 12-YEAR-OLD BOY

In November 2001, Howard Brooks, an aide to California Assemblyman Phil Wyman (R-Tehachapi), was arrested and charged with molesting a 12-year-old male child while he lived with Brooks and his wife. Wyman announced that he had requested that Brooks be fired by the Assembly Rules Committee.[98]

Brooks was arrested after prison authorities intercepted a letter that he sent to an inmate in which he described sexual abuse of boys including a seven-year-old in his neighborhood. No charges involving the seven-year-old were filed.[99]

In August 2002, Brooks pleaded no contest to a molestation charge and was sentenced to three years in prison.[100]

JURY FINDS ANTI-ABORTION ACTIVIST GUILTY OF MOLESTING GIRL AT HIS HOME FOR UNWED MOTHERS

In April 2004, controversial Florida anti-abortion leader John Allen Burt was found guilty of four counts of lewd or lascivious molestation and one count of lewd or lascivious conduct, after a 15-year-old girl residing in his home for unwed mothers accused him of fondling her and giving her a sexually explicit note. Burt was sentenced to 18 years in prison; he could have faced 75 years. Burt lost his appeal of the conviction in July 2005.[101]

When the warrant was issued for Burt's arrest, he fled town but was apprehended by police five days later. His family denied that he molested the teen. His adopted daughter, Karen Krzan, said:

"We're dealing with troubled teenage girls to begin with. If parents are sending them away from their house, it's generally for a good reason. . . . He's made enough people angry around here that anything they could get on him they would try."[102]

Burt had ties to violent anti-abortion protestors and was successfully sued by the family of a doctor murdered by an anti-abortion protestor.[103]

FORMER HAWAII COUNTY COUNCIL MEMBER ADMITS TO MOLESTING YOUNG MALE FAMILY MEMBER

In March 2000, Keola Childs was arrested for molesting a male family member under the age 14. Childs served on the Hawaii County Council from 1992 to 1996 as a Republican. In August 2000, Childs pleaded guilty to first-degree sexual assault of a juvenile family member and was sentenced to one year in jail and 20 years probation. Childs also had to register as a sex offender.[104]

CREATOR OF CONTROVERSIAL ANTI-GORE COMMERCIAL CONVICTED OF SEXUAL ASSAULT OF CHILD

In June 2006, a jury found Republican media consultant Carey Lee Cramer guilty on four counts of sexual assault of children. Two girls, who were 15-years-old at the time of the trial, accused Cramer of molesting them. One of the girls maintained that Cramer molested her over several years while she lived with him and his wife and that the molestation began when she was eight years old. Cramer claimed that the allegations were made up by his wife in order to win custody of their son.[105]

Cramer had created an anti-Gore television ad during the 2000 presidential race. The ad accused the Clinton-Gore administration of giving China nuclear technology in exchange for campaign contributions. It was modeled after the "Daisy" ad, which ran during the 1964 presidential campaign against Barry Goldwater. Cramer refused to reveal who had paid for the commercial.[106]

One of the girls who accused Cramer of molesting her appeared in the ad.[107]

CONNECTICUT SELECTMAN ACCUSED OF FONDLING 13-YEAR-OLD GIRL

In March 2004, Republican Stonington, Connecticut, First Selectman Peter Dibble was arrested for inappropriately touching and kissing a 13-year-old girl almost 40 times over a three-year period, beginning when she was ten. Dibble denied some of the accusations and maintained that the kissing was not sexual.[108]

Dibble initially refused to resign his office. Ultimately, the board agreed to pay him $81,000 in exchange for his resignation.[109]

In June 2004, Dibble pleaded no contest to a lesser misdemeanor of reckless endangerment. He was sentenced to two years of unsupervised probation. Because he pleaded to a misdemeanor, Dibble did not have to register as a sex offender. Dibble had been charged with risk of injury to a minor, for which he could have been sentenced to ten years in prison.[110]

REPUBLICAN PENNSYLVANIA BOROUGH COUNCILMAN ELECTED DESPITE HAVING SERVED JAIL TIME FOR CHILD MOLESTATION

In 2003, Millersville, Pennsylvania, Borough Councilman Jack W. Gardner was elected to office as a Republican despite the fact that he served time in prison in 1971 for molesting a 12-year-old girl at Millersville's Old Mill Inn.

Gardner was 24 when he went to prison. In 2003, Ron Harper, a constituent and publisher of 5thstate.com awarded Gardner the "golden plunger" at a council meeting and stated that he was unfit to serve as a public official because of his past crime. Gardner thanked Harper for the award and shook his hand.[111]

GOP committeewoman Ruth M. Feller defended Gardner, saying he had served his time and that Christians should "forgive and forget":

> *"At the time Mr. Gardner ran for office, we were told in no uncertain terms that while Jack had created a rather grievous situation, he had served his time to the people of Pennsylvania, and there was no way we could prevent him from running for borough council. Jack has been elected time after time, and he has served with honor. We're supposed to be Christians and to forgive and forget. It's time to put this to rest."*[112]

MAN WHO LED CRUSADE AGAINST GAY ADOPTION SUPPORTED BY REPUBLICAN OFFICIALS MOLESTS ADOPTED DAUGHTER

In May 1999, Earl "Butch" Kimmerling was arrested for molesting his adopted daughter. The girl told Kimmerling's wife, Sandy, that he was molesting her, and the mother reported it to the police, who confirmed that secretions on the girl's bed matched Kimmerling's DNA. The molestation charges came after the

Kimmerlings had waged a public battle against the girl's adoption by a gay man who was adopting her three brothers. In order to prevent the adoption, the Kimmerlings adopted the girl, who was their foster child at the time.[113]

In January 2000, Kimmerling was sentenced to 40 years in prison after pleading guilty to four counts of child molestation.[114]

Indiana Republican state representatives Woody Burton and Jack Lutz, as well as Anderson Mayor Mark Lawler, supported the Kimmerlings in their efforts to prevent their foster daughter's adoption by a gay man. Kimmerling called the man's home "immoral."[115]

OWNER OF REPUBLICAN PETITION BUSINESS CONVICTED OF MOLESTING TWO TEENS

In a May 2006 story on the access that petition workers have to people's personal information and the lack of scrutiny required of petition workers, the *Orange County Register* interviewed Tom Randall, the owner of the petition business Orange Coast. Randall noted that it was hard to find people to gather signatures who "should be out there representing the Republican Party."[116]

The paper also noted that Randall pleaded guilty in 2002 to molesting two girls under the age of 14, one of whom was the daughter of a business associate, and served 188 days in Orange County Jail and 83 days on a work crew at Mason Regional Park in Irvine.[117]

CHAIR OF SOUTH CAROLINA LOCAL CHRISTIAN COALITION AND STATE GOP EXECUTIVE COMMITTEE MEMBER ADMITS TO SEXUALLY MOLESTING HIS STEPDAUGHTER, CHILD KILLER SUSAN SMITH

In 1995, during the high-profile murder trial of South Carolinian Susan Smith, Smith's stepfather, Beverly C. Russell, admitted that he had molested his stepdaughter and had sexual relations with her three weeks before she killed her two young sons. Smith had told the police that he began molesting her when she was 15 years old.[118]

Russell was the chairman of the Union County, South Carolina, Republican Party and head of the Union County Christian Coalition prior to his stepdaughter's arrest. He continued to serve on the state's Republican executive committee for six months following his daughter's revelation of her molestation.[119]

Three months after Smith's conviction, Russell was nominated as a delegate to the Union County Republican Party Convention and called "a man of integrity" at a Promise Keepers rally.[120] According to the *Orlando Sentinel*, one fellow Republican said:

> *"I think he ought to be allowed to be back in the community in a place of leadership. He's trying to make right the areas (where) he has made mistakes in the past."*[121]

Four Years Later, Mother of Illegitimate Son Asked Court to Continue Prohibiting Unsupervised Visitations, Cites Molestation of Smith, "Obsessed with Pornography"

In June 1999, the *Greenville News* reported that a judge had continued an earlier order to restrict Russell to only supervised visits with his illegitimate two-year-old son. The boy's mother, Cheryl Tate, asked the court to deny unsupervised visits because

Russell was "an admitted pedophile" and was "obsessed with pornography."[122]

KENTUCKY REPUBLICAN COUNTY CHAIR ARRESTED FOR SEXUAL ABUSE OF FIVE-YEAR-OLD BOY

In October 2005, former Floyd County, Kentucky, Republican Party Chair Robert "Bobby" Stumbo was arrested and charged with sexually abusing a five-year-old boy. Stumbo ran unsuccessfully as a Republican for state representative in 2004. The boy's mother filed the complaint with the police. Stumbo was a friend of the mother's former husband.[123]

REPUBLICAN PARTY CHAIRMAN, NEW YORK COUNTY GOP CHAIR, AND ELECTIONS COMMISSIONER, PLEADS GUILTY TO LESSER CHARGE AFTER ACCUSED OF MOLESTING 14-YEAR-OLD

In June 2006, Schenectady County, New York, Republican Party Chair and Elections Commissioner Armando Tebano was arrested for molesting a 14-year-old girl while watching *Star Wars* at his home. The girl initially made a statement to the sheriff in August 2005, two days after the incident, but no charges were filed. Later, her parents had the case referred to the Montgomery County prosecutor and charges were filed in June 2006.[124]

Tebano's wife, County Judge Karen Drago, stood by him through the proceedings.[125]

Tebano was charged with third-degree sexual abuse, forcible touching, and child endangerment, all misdemeanors.[126]

During the preparations for trial, the prosecutor was unsuccessful in his attempts to enter into evidence four prior incidents that he asserted showed bad behavior. In one, the prosecutor

65

claimed Tebano took "nearly nude" pictures of three underage girls.[127]

In February 2007, Tebano pleaded guilty to a lesser charge of harassment. He was fined $250 and sentenced to 250 hours of community service. Tebano could have spent up to a year in jail if he had been found guilty of the original charges.[128]

SEE ALSO:

Richard Gardner Jr., Republican Candidate for Nevada Assembly (Incest)

Judge Ronald C. Kline (Child Pornography)

CHILD PORNOGRAPHY

GREEN OAKS, ILLINOIS, GOP MAYOR CHARGED WITH DISTRIBUTING CHILD PORNOGRAPHY

In July 2006, Green Oaks, Illinois, Mayor Tom Adams was arrested for distributing child pornography over the Internet. Adams served as chairman of the Lake County Republican Party from 2002 to 2004. Adams was charged with 16 counts of distribution of child pornography and 17 counts of possession of child pornography.[129]

In July 2007, the Republican judge presiding over Adams' case recused herself after receiving a message from a Democratic councilman urging her not to accept a plea deal from Adams that was too lenient. Adams was facing a mandatory prison sentence of up to 15 years.[130]

In September 2007, Adams sought to have his case dismissed, claiming that he could not receive a fair trial.[131]

"REPUBLICAN ACTIVIST" AND BUSH ELECTOR SENTENCED TO FEDERAL PRISON FOR POSSESSION OF CHILD PORNOGRAPHY

In November 2001, Parker J. Bena, a "Republican activist" and one of Virginia's 13 electors, pleaded guilty to one count of possession of child pornography. The original indictment against Bena included nine counts. Under the plea agreement, Bena was sentenced to 30 months in federal prison, was required to pay an $18,000 fine, and was put on three years probation.[132]

At least eight pictures of nude boys and girls engaging in sexual acts were found on Bena's computer, including one of a child under the age of three. Bena was also charged with lying to the FBI about the crimes.[133]

In 2000, the Associated Press asked Bena if he would consider changing his electoral vote to reflect the fact that Gore had won the popular vote. Bena said he was "sticking with" Bush:

"No way, I am not changing my vote. I'm sticking with the man I believe in and that is George W. Bush. The voters of this Commonwealth charged me with casting their vote and I'm going to do just that!"[134]

GOP ACTIVIST, FUND-RAISER, COMMENTATOR, CONVICTED OF TAKING LEWD PHOTOS OF 16-YEAR-OLD GIRL

In 2003, Richard A. Delgaudio "was sentenced to two years' probation after he admitted to taking lewd photographs of a 16-year-old girl he met in East Baltimore's Patterson Park in 2001." The *Washington Post* called Delgaudio "a longtime Northern Virginia-based fundraiser for conservative causes and personalities."[135]

At the time, Delgaudio was president of the Legal Affairs Council, which had provided financial assistance to Oliver North and Caspar Weinberger with their legal bills for the Iran-

Contra affair. Delgaudio was a "frequent talk-radio guest" who had called President Clinton, in the wake of the Lewinsky affair, a "lawbreaker and terrible example to our nation's young people."[136]

According to a statement by Delgaudio's attorneys, Delgaudio:

> *"Acknowledges the acute moral shortcomings of his conduct and he will continue intense self-examination, and professional and spiritual counseling."*[137]

REPUBLICAN JUDGE SENTENCED TO 27 MONTHS IN FEDERAL PRISON FOR POSSESSING CHILD PORNOGRAPHY

In February 2007, former Orange County, California, Judge Ronald C. Kline was sentenced to 27 months in federal prison for possession of child pornography. In addition, Kline was given three years probation, ordered to register as a sex offender, and prohibited from "lingering" within 100 feet of schools, parks, or other gathering places for children.[138]

Kline had agreed to a plea deal in which he admitted to four counts of possession of child pornography.[139]

Kline was arrested in November 2001 but his case had many appeals, including whether the evidence collected by a computer hacker of more than 1,500 pornographic images of young male children on his home and courthouse computers was admissible. Following his arrest, Kline claimed a sex addiction and entered a treatment facility. While at the facility, he allegedly pursued an 18-year-old disabled man even though he was ordered to stay away from the teenager.[140]

An assistant U.S. attorney warned that authorities were worried about whether Kline might pose a risk upon his eventual release "given the writings in his diary," which "contained accounts of him following children in shopping malls and being attracted to boys when he worked as a volunteer baseball umpire."[141]

After Kline was arrested, a former neighbor came forward and claimed that Kline molested him as a young boy 25 years earlier. The case was ultimately dismissed due to the statute of limitations.[142]

Kline was appointed to the Orange County Superior Court in 1995 and was running unopposed as a Republican for re-election when he was arrested.[143]

STATE DELEGATE RESIGNS AFTER CHILD PORNOGRAPHY INVESTIGATION

In January 2008, officials conducting a child-porn sting removed several computers, videotapes, and printed material from the home of Maryland State Delegate Robert McKee. He promptly resigned his office, as well as his position with the Big Brothers/ Big Sisters program.[144]

In a letter published by the *Hagerstown Herald-Mail*, McKee confirmed that the seizure was related to "images that are available on the Internet," said it was "deeply embarrassing," and claimed he was entering treatment.[145]

ANTI-ABORTION ACTIVIST WHO POSTED $1.5 MILLION BOUNTY FOR DEATH OF ABORTION DOCTOR SENTENCED TO PRISON FOR BOUNTY AND POSSESSION OF CHILD PORN

In June 2001, Nicholas Morency was sentenced to 30 months in federal prison and required to register as a sex offender after he pleaded guilty to offering a $1.5 million bounty for the killing of a Kansas abortion doctor and to possessing child pornography. According to prosecutors, Morency possessed more than 1,000 images of child pornography and some of the images were of children as young as five years old.[146]

MUNICIPAL GOP MEMBER ARRESTED FOR DOWNLOADING VIDEO CLIP OF RAPE OF FIVE-YEAR-OLD

In February 2005, Jeffrey Patti, the chairman of the Sparta, New Jersey, Municipal Republican Committee, was arrested for downloading a video clip of a five-year-old girl being raped. Patti was caught along with 35 others in a sting operation. Patti resigned his position following his arrest but later said that he wished to remain on the committee, as he was innocent of the charges. At the time, Patti was married with two young daughters.[147]

In April 2006, a judge ruled that Patti could enter the New Jersey pretrial intervention program, which allowed him not to have to plead guilty to the charges and also required the dismissal of all charges at the completion of the program. The judge claimed that the program was similar to the sentence he would receive under a fourth-degree crime. Patti was originally charged with distribution of child pornography but the charge was dropped.[148]

The judge claimed that Patti's participation in therapy following his offense was an admission of having viewed the clip:

"He's highly motivated and disturbed by his behavior."[149]

CALIFORNIA POLITICAL CONSULTANT ARRESTED FOR TAKING PHOTOS OF PARTIALLY CLOTHED TEENAGED GIRLS

In 2001, Republican political consultant Thomas Percy Shortridge pleaded no contest to misdemeanor criminal charges associated with photos he took of two partially nude teenaged girls. Shortridge had previously pleaded not guilty to felony charges of using a minor for sex acts and child molesting. The felony charges were dropped as part of the plea deal. Shortridge was put on three years' probation, ordered to do 200 hours of community service and to continue counseling, and prohibited from associating with girls under the age of 18 without a parent present.[150]

According to the *Daily Breeze*, Shortridge had worked with "more than two-dozen local politicians" prior to his criminal conviction.[151]

Prior to the plea deal, Shortridge's attorney claimed that the girls had asked Shortridge to take modeling photos of them and that they had brought the "skimpy clothing" with them to the shoot.[152]

SEE ALSO:

Constable Larry Dale Floyd, Denton County, Texas
    (Enticement)

State Legislator Ted Klaudt (R-SD) **(Rape)**

State Representative Larry Jack Schwarz (R-CO)
    *(*Pornography*)*

CHILD SUPPORT, UNPAID

U.S. Representative Bob Barr (R-GA) (see **Impeachment, Advocates of Clinton's**)

U.S. Representative Newt Gingrich (R-GA) (see **Gingrich Family Values**)

DA Mark Pazuhanich (Monroe County, PA) (see **Fondling**)

CHOKING

REPUBLICAN CONGRESSMAN ADMITS EXTRAMARITAL AFFAIR WITH WOMAN 30 YEARS YOUNGER AFTER POLICE RESPONDED TO CALL HE WAS CHOKING HER

In September 2004, Washington, D.C., police responded to a domestic abuse call from the apartment of U.S. Representative Don Sherwood (R-PA). According to the police report, Cynthia Ore told them that Sherwood "choked her for no apparent reason" while giving her a back rub. The police noted that Sherwood and Ore both confirmed that he was giving her a back rub but that Sherwood denied trying to choke her. No arrest was made.[153]

Nine months later, the Wilkes-Barre *Times Leader* reported on the incident. In an interview, Ore told the paper that Sherwood had promised to get a divorce but later said he had to stay married in order to remain in Congress:

> *"He never did get a divorce. He said he has to stay married to get elected."*[154]

In 2005, Ore filed a lawsuit against Sherwood claiming that he "brutally assaulted and struck her on several occasions" during their five-year affair. Ore asked for $5.5 million in damages.[155]

Ore claimed that she met Sherwood at a Young Republicans event and that she lived with Sherwood in his apartment while he was in Washington, D.C. Ore maintained that she continued in the relationship with Sherwood, despite the abuse, because he promised to marry her and start a family.[156]

Sherwood settled the suit for an undisclosed amount.[157]

After the allegations against Sherwood became the subject of a campaign commercial by his opponent, Sherwood's wife, Carol, wrote a letter to constituents defending her husband:

"Chris Carney might be trying to make himself look squeaky clean, but we have all made mistakes we regret over the years. I am certainly not condoning the mistake Don made, but I'm not going to dwell on it, either."[158]

While campaigning for Sherwood, President Bush claimed he was "deeply moved" by the letter:

"Carol's letter shows what a caring and courageous woman she is."[159]

Sherwood also ran a commercial in which he directly apologized for his actions, saying:

"I made a mistake that nearly cost me the love of my wife, Carol, and our daughters. As a family, we've worked through this. Should you forgive me, you can count on me to continue to fight for you and your family."[160]

CHRISTIAN DUTY

U.S. Senator Bob Packwood (R-OR) (see **Harassment, Sexual**)

CLOSET(ED)

State Representative Bob Allen (R-FL) (see **Men's Rooms**)

U.S. Representative Robert Bauman (R-MD) (see **Soliciting Sex w/ a Minor**)

U.S. Senator Larry Craig (R-ID) (see **Men's Rooms**)

State Senator Richard Curtis (R-WA) (see **Prostitution**)

Councilman Joey DiFatta (St. Bernard Parish, LA) (see **Men's Rooms**)

Republican County Chairman Donald Fleischman (Brown County, WI) (see **Fondling**)

U.S. Representative Mark Foley (R-FL) (see **Pages, Congressional**)

Rev. Ted Haggard (see **Prostitution**)

Glenn Murphy, Jr., President of the Young Republican National Federation (see **Unwanted Sex Acts**)

State Representative Brent Parker (R-UT) (see **Groping of Law Enforcement Officials**)

U.S. Representative Ed Schrock (R-VA) (see **Telephone Dating Service**)

Mayor Jim West (Spokane, WA) (see **Chat Room**)

Stephen White, Conservative Activist (see **Soliciting Sex w/ a Minor**)

COKE CAN

Supreme Court Justice Clarence Thomas (see **Harassment, Sexual**)

COUSINS

Mayor Rudy Giuliani (New York, NY) (see **Adultery**)

"Who has put pubic hair on my Coke?"
—*Justice Clarence Thomas*

CROSS-DRESSING

FEDERAL JUDGE, IN DRAG, ARRESTED FOR DRUNK DRIVING

In February 2008, Judge Robert Somma, a President Bush appointee, was arrested for drunk driving. When he stepped out of his vehicle, he was wearing a cocktail dress, fishnet stockings, and high heels. The officer noted that Somma had a hard time locating his driver's license in his purse.[161]

STATE REPRESENTATIVE CANDIDATE ADMITS TO DRESSING IN WOMEN'S CLOTHING

In 2004, just days before he faced voters in a run-off for the Texas State legislature, photos surfaced of the frontrunner, 64-year-old businessman Sam Walls, wearing women's clothing.[162]

SEE ALSO:

State Senator Richard Curtis (R-WA) **(Prostitution)**

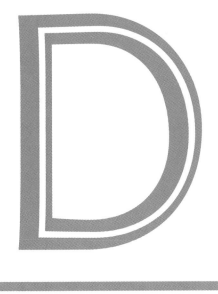

"Every day of my life I pray for those who are the victims of sexual abuse."[163]

—NICHOLAS MORENCY, Conservative Activist

DELINQUENCY OF A MINOR, CONTRIBUTING TO

CONGRESSMAN FORCED TO RESIGN AFTER CONVICTED OF HAVING SEX WITH 16-YEAR-OLD, ALSO ACCUSED OF FONDLING CAPITOL ELEVATOR OPERATOR

In June 1989, a jury convicted U.S. Representative Donald "Buz" Lukens (R-OH) of contributing to the unruliness of a minor. Rosie Coffman claimed that Lukens paid her $40 to have sex with him in 1988 when she was 16 years old. Coffman later claimed that she also had sex with Lukens in 1984 when she was 14 years old. Lukens was sentenced to 30 days in jail and a $500 fine.[164]

Coffman sued Lukens twice for damages involving their sexual encounter.[165]

Lukens lost re-election in the Republican primary in 1990.[166]

Lukens resigned his seat in 1990, prior to the end of his term, after the House Ethics Committee voted to investigate allegations that he fondled a House elevator operator.[167]

Later Convicted of Taking Bribe, Went to Federal Prison, Claimed Money was Loan to Pay Lawyers on Sex Charge

In 1996, Lukens was sentenced to 30 months in federal prison for accepting $15,000 in bribes from the operators of an Ohio trade school chain. Lukens claimed he thought the money was a loan to pay his creditors and the lawyer who represented him on the sex charges.[168]

LONGTIME NEW HAMPSHIRE REPUBLICAN CAMPAIGN AIDE WITH PRIOR SEX OFFENSE CONVICTIONS ARRESTED AGAIN FOR ASKING MALE TEEN TO "PARTY" IN EXCHANGE FOR ALCOHOL

In 2005, Mark Seidensticker, a longtime campaign aide to New Hampshire Executive Councilor Raymond Burton, was arrested for offering beer and cigarettes to a 14-year-old boy. The boy claimed that Seidensticker seemed like a "pervert" and that he thought Seidensticker wanted sexual favors from him. Seidensticker ultimately agreed to a deal where he pleaded guilty to charges of offering beer and cigarettes to a minor, in exchange for the maximum sentence (one year) and a $3,000 fine. The deal did not include a two-year probation requirement, which had been set by a lower court judge.[169]

After Seidensticker's arrest, the *Union Leader* reported that Seidensticker had been convicted of prior sexual offenses involving teenagers. In 1994, he was convicted of attempted sexual assault when he grabbed a 17-year-old boy from behind, pulled him to the ground and pressed his exposed genitals against the boy's "buttocks area."[170] He was also convicted of violating a protective order taken out by his ex-boyfriend and of failing to register as a sex offender in Maine.[171]

Burton admitted that he knew about Seidensticker's past and took precautions to protect children:

> *"I made it very clear there was to be no contact with children. When he was with me, he was under my strict supervision."*[172]

However, Burton acknowledged that he did not know the extent of Seidensticker's criminal history:

> *"I knew it was sort of somewhere in the background, but the details, I was unaware of."*[173]

SEE ALSO:

Republican Party Chairman Donald Fleischman (Brown County, WI) **(Fondling)**

DILDO

Rev. Gary M. Aldridge (see **Asphyxiation, Autoerotic**)

Bill O'Reilly, FOX News Commentator (see **Harassment, Sexual**)

DORA THE EXPLORER

Federal Prosecutor John David "Roy" Atchison (R–FL) (see **Soliciting Sex w/ a Minor**)

DRAMAMINE

State Senator Galen Fox (R–HI) (see **Groping**)

DRUGS

Randal David Ankeney, Employee of Governor Bill Owens (*see* **Assault, Sexual**)

Marty Glickman, Conservative Commentator (see **Unlawful Sexual Activity**)

Mayor John Gosek (Oswego, NY) (see **Soliciting Sex w/ a Minor**)

Rev. Ted Haggard (see **Prostitution**)

"I'm a lot more like Lorena Bobbitt than Hillary. If [Senator David Vitter] does anything like that, I'm walking away with one thing, and it's not alimony, trust me."[174]

—WENDY VITTER, Wife of Senator David Vitter (R–LA)

ENTICEMENT

REPUBLICAN TEXAS CONSTABLE CONVICTED FOR SOLICITING SEX WITH EIGHT-YEAR-OLD GIRL AND POSSESSING CHILD PORNOGRAPHY

In July 2005, Denton County, Texas, constable Larry Dale Floyd was arrested in Colorado after he solicited sex with an eight-year-old girl and her mother over the Internet. The mother, who was actually an undercover officer, had also agreed to arrange for Floyd to have sex with a friend's 16-month old and three-year-old.[175]

According to the undercover officer, Floyd wanted to have sex with the younger children because they would not be able to tell about what had happened:

"He mentioned a few times that they were the age that they wouldn't talk and tell and asked if I thought they would. I told him that they wouldn't."[176]

Floyd had been a Denton County, Texas, constable since 1993, and is registered as a Republican.[177]

After Floyd's arrest, the Colony police department reported that they had investigated him for molesting two relatives in 2002 but that the statute of limitations prevented them from filing charges.[178]

Floyd's cellmate told authorities that Floyd admitted to paying for sex with Vietnamese children while he served in the U.S. Army and told the cellmate that he and his fellow officers had chained up a child, repeatedly had sex with her, and then killed her.[179]

In January 2007, Floyd was sentenced to six-years to life after he pleaded guilty to three charges of enticement of a child. Although Floyd could be eligible for parole after six years, Kathy Eberling, the Colorado prosecutor who handled the case, noted that Colorado's tough sex offender laws rarely released offenders on their initial opportunity for parole. According to Eberling:

> *"The likelihood is that he'll be in prison for a really long time."*[180]

In September 2007, Floyd pleaded guilty to three counts of possession of child pornography brought against him by Denton County authorities. The pornography was found after a search of his house following his arrest in Colorado. He was sentenced to three concurrent ten-year sentences to begin after he serves his Colorado prison time.[181]

ESCORT

CONSERVATIVE WHITE HOUSE REPORTER FORCED TO RESIGN AFTER BLOGGERS REVEAL WEB SITE OFFERING HIS SERVICES AS GAY ESCORT

In February 2005, Jeff Gannon, a White House reporter for Talon News and GOPUSA, both funded by a Texas Republican activist, was forced to resign after liberal bloggers revealed that he was using a pseudonym and that he had posted naked pictures of himself in order to promote his services as a $200-per-hour gay escort. The bloggers investigated Gannon, whose real name is James Dale Guckert, after he asked a "loaded question" of President Bush during a news conference that contained false information about Democratic leaders:[182]

> *"Senate Democratic leaders have painted a very bleak picture of the U.S. economy. [Minority Leader] Harry Reid was talking about soup lines, and Hillary Clinton was talking about the economy being on the verge of collapse. Yet, in the same breath, they say that Social Security is rock solid and there's*

no crisis there. How are you going to work—you said you're going to reach out to these people—how are you going to work with people who seem to have divorced themselves from reality?"[183]

Hotmilitarystud.com, Militaryescorts.com, and Militaryescorts-m4m.com were three of the Web domains owned by Gannon.[184]

White House Press Secretary Scott McClellan denied that Gannon had a permanent press pass, which would have required a background check, and instead said he was let into the press room on a day-to-day basis.[185]

Gannon denied getting special treatment from the White House, saying the suggestion was "absolutely, completely, totally untrue."[186]

EXHIBITIONISM
(see **Indecent Exposure**)

EXTREME CRUELTY

CALIFORNIA CONGRESSMAN
ACCUSED BY WIFE OF PHYSICAL ABUSE
AND "EXTREME CRUELTY"

Between 1960 and 1976, the wife of former congressman and presidential candidate Bob Dornan filed four separate divorce actions against her husband. She alleged "physical abuse" and "extreme cruelty." She once took out a restraining order against him after he had "pull[ed] her through the house by the hair, produc[ed] a revolver and pour[ed] a quart of milk over her head."[187]

During his 1996 congressional race against Democrat Loretta Sanchez, Dornan predicted, "She can't beat me. . . . Bob Dornan is a father of five, grandfather of 10, military man, been married 41 years. She has no kids, no military, no track record. I win."

Dornan lost that race by just under 1,000 votes.[188]

"The statute of limitations has long since passed on my youthful indiscretions."[189]

—Representative HENRY HYDE (R-IL)

FALAFEL

Bill O'Reilly, FOX News Commentator (see **Harassment, Sexual**)

FAITH AND FAMILY ALLIANCE

Robin Vanderwall, Conservative Activist (see **Soliciting Sex w/ a Minor**)

FATHER/SON BONDING

FUTURE PRESIDENT CRUDELY ADMITS THE CONTENT OF CONVERSATIONS WITH HIS FATHER

At the 1988 Republican National Convention, when George H. W. Bush was running for president of the United States, future president George W. Bush was asked by a *Hartford Courant* reporter what he and his father talked about when they weren't talking about politics.

Bush's answer: "Pussy."[190]

FINANCIAL PAYMENTS

Attorney General Mike Bowers (R-GA) (see **Adultery**)

F

FOOT SIGNALS

(see **Men's Rooms**)

FONDLING

GOP COUNTY CHAIR IN WISCONSIN
ACCUSED OF FONDLING TEENAGE RUNAWAY,
BUYING HIM BEER AND DRUGS

In September 2007, Donald Fleischman, the chair of the Brown County, Wisconsin, Republican Party, was charged with two counts of child enticement, two counts of contributing to the delinquency of a minor, and one count of exposing himself to a child. The maximum sentence is 52 years if convicted on all counts.[191]

Police officers went to Fleischman's home looking for a 16-year-old runaway from Ethan House, a juvenile home. They found the Fleischman's home, wearing only underwear and a T-shirt, and found evidence of marijuana and underage drinking. The boy told police that Fleischman had fondled him, taken him to hotels, and provided him with beer and marijuana.[192]

Fleischman's attorney maintained his client's innocence:

"My client is innocent of the charges. Our plan is to get some witnesses to testify and present enough information to dismiss the case."[193]

A preliminary hearing is set for April 22, 2008.[194]

REPUBLICAN DA AND JUDGE-ELECT PLEADS GUILTY TO FONDLING TEN-YEAR-OLD GIRL AT CONCERT, BANNED FOR LIFE FROM SERVICE AS JUDGE, DISBARRED

In November 2003, Monroe County, Pennsylvania, District Attorney and Judge-Elect Mark Pazuhanich was arrested for public drunkenness following a Hillary Duff concert. After the arrest, Pazuhanich checked himself into an alcohol rehabilitation center. Three weeks later, he was charged with molesting his ten-year-old daughter, who was sitting next to him at the concert.[195]

In the wake of his arrest, a judge suspended Pazuhanich's rights to see his daughter, who lived in New Jersey with her mother but visited frequently.[196]

According to the victim, Pazuhanich repeatedly touched her breasts and crotch despite her asking him to stop. Other witnesses, including the head of Duff's security, testified they witnessed Pazuhanich fondle the girl.[197]

Although Pazuhanich "vigorously" declared his innocence in January 2004, in July 2004, he pleaded no contest to two counts of indecent assault, one count of endangering the welfare of children, one count of corruption of a minor, and one count of public drunkenness. He was sentenced to probation and required to register as a sex offender for ten years. At the hearing, Pazuhanich told the judge that he understood that the no-contest plea meant that he was admitting his guilt.[198]

After his no-contest plea, Pazuhanich filed for bankruptcy, claiming debts including unpaid child support, was barred for life from serving as a judge in Pennsylvania, and was disbarred.[199]

Drew National Attention as DA after Seeking to Try Nine-Year-Old as Adult

According to the *Morning Call*, as district attorney, Pazuhanich "drew national attention" when he sought to try as an adult a nine-year-old boy who shot and killed his seven-year-old neighbor. The case ultimately went to juvenile court and the charges were dropped to involuntary manslaughter.[200]

SEE ALSO:

Randal David Ankeney, Employee of Governor Bill Owens **(Assault, Sexual)**

U.S. Representative Donald "Buz" Lukens (R-OH) **(Delinquency of a Minor, Contributing to)**

Governor Arnold Schwarzenegger (R-CA) **(Groping)**

FORGIVENESS, DIVINE

U.S. Representative Helen Chenoweth (R-ID) (see **Adultery**)

U.S. Representative Daniel Crane (R-IL) (see **Pages, Congressional**)

Councilman Jack W. Gardner (Millersville, PA) (see **Child Molestation**)

Rev. Ted Haggard (see **Prostitution**)

U.S. Senator David Vitter (R-LA) (see **Prostitution**)

FORGIVENESS, GUBERNATORIAL

ARKANSAS GOVERNOR ADVOCATES FOR RAPIST'S RELEASE; AFTER HIS RELEASE THE MAN RAPES AND KILLS AGAIN

As Arkansas governor, Mike Huckabee played a controversial role in the release of convicted rapist and murderer Wayne Dumond. When elected in 1996, a group of Huckabee's campaign supporters lobbied him to free Dumond because his victim, high school cheerleader Ashley Stevens, had been a distant cousin of Bill Clinton and the daughter of a major Clinton contributor. They considered the sentence for her killer too harsh, given her ties to the hated former governor who now occupied the White House. [201]

Dumond's case was championed by Huckabee's close friend, Baptist minister and radio host Jay Cole. According to parole board members, the new governor supported the cause and exerted pressure on them to intercede. [202]

Dumond subsequently raped and killed a Missouri woman after being released from Arkansas prison. [203]

"None of us could've predicted what [Dumond] could've done when he got out," Huckabee said, even though several of Dumond's past victims provided the governor with letters describing his crimes against them and imploring him not to commute the sentence. Huckabee also had access to the police reports, including one particularly disturbing episode in which a woman was raped at knifepoint with her baby in the bed next to her. [204]

Huckabee refused to accept any responsibility, but others with knowledge of the case disagreed:

"I signed the [parole] papers because the governor wanted Dumond paroled," said Ermer Pondexter, an ex-member of the board of pardons and paroles who also confirmed that Huckabee met with the board privately to discuss the case. "I was thinking the governor was working for the best interests of the state."[205]

FORGIVENESS, SPOUSAL

Attorney General Mike Bowers (R-GA) (see **Adultery**)

Rev. Ted Haggard (see **Prostitution**)

State Representative Brent Parker (R-UT) (see **Groping of Law Enforcement Officials**)

U.S. Representative Don Sherwood (R-PA) (see **Choking**)

U.S. Senator David Vitter (R-LA) (see **Prostitution**)

FRIENDLY BEHAVIOR

State Representative S. Vance Wilkins (R-VA)
(see **Harassment, Sexual**)

*"When you see a blonde with great tits
and a great ass, you say to yourself,
'Hey, she must be stupid or must have
nothing else to offer,' which maybe is
the case many times."*[206]

—Governor ARNOLD SCHWARZENEGGER (R-CA)

GAY ADOPTION OPPOSITION

Earl "Butch" Kimmerling, Conservative Activist (see **Child Molestation**)

GINGRICH FAMILY VALUES

SPEAKER OF THE HOUSE MARRIED HIGH SCHOOL MATH TEACHER AT 19 YEARS OLD, HAD TWO CHILDREN, WIFE SUPPORTED HIM THOUGH COLLEGE, GRADUATE SCHOOL, AND EARLY CAMPAIGNS

In 1962, at the age of 19, Newt Gingrich married his high school geometry teacher, Jackie Battley. Battley was seven years older than Gingrich. The couple had a daughter nine months later and another daughter three years after that. None of Gingrich's family attended the wedding, which his stepfather, Bob Gingrich, vehemently opposed.[207]

In 1985, Gingrich said his first marriage made sense at the time:

> *"Jackie was my math teacher in high school and it really made a tremendous amount of sense to marry at the time, when I was a freshman in college. Who you are at 19 may not be who you are at 39. We were married not quite a year when Kathy was born, so I had a daughter in my sophomore year of college with all the economic pressures that implies, and then Jackie Sue was born when I was in graduate school."*[208]

"I saw . . . one of the guys' wives with her head in his lap going up and down. Newt kind of turned and gave me his little boy smile."
—*former Gingrich campaign aide*

According to Dolores Adamson, Gingrich's district administrator in the late 1970s and early 1980s, Jackie financially supported Gringrich:

> *"Jackie put him all the way through school. All the way through the P.h.D. . . . He didn't work."*[209]

According to a profile in the *Washington Post*, the Gingrichs' friends characterized Jackie as a "cross between a mother and a wife":

> *"The couple's friends said Jackie Gingrich seemed like a cross between a mother and a wife, with Newt usually seeking her advice before making decisions and Jackie counseling him like a student. They were loving, always holding hands in public."*[210]

Gingrich Went to Congress by Touting Role as Family Man, 18 Months Later Divorced Wife, Forced Her to Discuss Details in Hospital while Recovering from Cancer Treatment

During his successful 1978 campaign for Congress, Gingrich ran ads against his opponent, Virginia Shapard, in which he claimed that he would "keep his family together" if he won the election, unlike his female opponent, who planned to commute to work so as not to uproot her family.[211]

Eighteen months later, Gingrich told his wife that he was filing for divorce.[212]

Gingrich Claimed Discussed Divorce with Wife for Ten Years, Wife Says Divorce was "Complete Surprise,"

In 1985, Gingrich told the *Washington Post* that he and Jackie had considered divorcing for ten years:

> *"I think the most diplomatic thing to say is I understand what they mean when they say irreconcilable differences. We had been talking about it off and on since 1969. I am a very shy*

*person. I had not dated much when I met her. I think I was
very lonely and I think I was very driven . . . If you decide in
your freshman year in high school that your job is to spend
your lifetime trying to change the future of your people, you're
probably fairly weird. I think I was pretty weird as a kid."*[213]

Jackie claimed that Gingrich's desire to divorce was a "complete surprise" and described his visit to her in the hospital to discuss the details of their divorce while she was recovering from uterine cancer surgery:

*"He can say that we had been talking about it for 10 years,
but the truth is that it came as a complete surprise. He's a
great wordsmith . . . He walked out in the spring of 1980
and I returned to Georgia. By September, I went into the
hospital for my third surgery. The two girls came to see me,
and said Daddy is downstairs and could he come up? When
he got there, he wanted to discuss the terms of the divorce
while I was recovering from the surgery . . . To say I gave up a
lot for the marriage is the understatement of the year."*[214]

In 1984, Lee Howell, a friend of Gingrich's, described the hospital incident to *Mother Jones*:

*"Newt came up there with his yellow legal pad, and he had a
list of things on how the divorce was going to be handled. He
wanted her to sign it. She was still recovering from surgery,
still sort of out of it, and he comes in with a yellow sheet of
paper, handwritten, and wants her to sign it."*[215]

When the *Washington Post* asked Gingrich whether "he handled the divorce as insensitively as portrayed," he said:

*"All I can say is when you have been talking about divorce
for 11 years and you've gone to a marriage counselor, and the
other person doesn't want the divorce, I'm not sure there is
any sensitive way to handle it."*[216]

Friend Says Gingrich Thought Jackie Was Too Frumpy for Washington

In a 1984 *Mother Jones* profile, Howell, who had worked as a press secretary during early Gingrich campaigns, claimed Gingrich saw Jackie as a liability:

> *"Jackie was kind of frumpy. She's lost a lot of weight now, but she was kind of frumpy in Washington, and she was seven years older than he was. And I guess Newt thought, well, it doesn't look good for an articulate, young, aggressive, attractive congressman to have a frumpy old wife."*[217]

Former Campaign Worker Claims Gingrich Said Jackie Not Pretty Enough to Be President's Wife; Gingrich Claims Man Disgruntled Worker Who Was Fired

In 1994, L. H. "Kip" Carter, who served as Gingrich's campaign treasurer in his early campaigns, claimed that Gingrich told him that Jackie was not pretty enough to be his wife. According to Carter, Gingrich said:

> *"She's not young enough or pretty enough to be the wife of the president. And besides, she has cancer."*[218]

In response to the allegation, Gingrich claimed that Carter was fired and that his allegations were false:

> *"This is a guy I deliberately fired because we got into an argument about whether or not he had to tell me what he was doing. If you could cross-reference every person quoted in every one of these articles [about his divorce], they're almost always the same three people. . . . So here's this image that on the one hand, Gingrich really sheds people, except by the way, there are people now who have worked with him for a quarter century. Now which is true?"*[219]

Carter claimed that he resigned.[220]

Divorce Court Filings Revealed Failure to Adequately Support Children, Church Had to Take Up Collection for Family

According to court papers filed during Gingrich's first divorce, Gingrich was paying his wife $400 a month in support in addition to $40 each for his daughters' monthly allowances. According to local papers, Jackie could not pay her basic household bills and was in danger of having her utilities cut off. Members of her church took up a collection to help her "make ends meet." After Gingrich provided the judge overseeing the case with an accounting of his monthly expenses, which included $400 for "food/dry cleaning etc.," the judge ordered Gingrich to pay more.[221]

Nine Years Later, Called First Divorce "a Tragedy," Said Never Spoke Badly of Ex-Wife

In 1994, Gingrich called his divorce of Jackie "a tragedy":

"We had been through counseling in the 1970s. It didn't work. It was a tragedy. I wish it had not happened. I mean you go through life and sometimes things happen. . . . In a different world maybe it would have worked differently. And I never speak ill of my ex-wife. She raised two wonderful daughters."[222]

Former Campaign Workers Reported Affairs During First Marriage

A 1984 profile of Gingrich in *Mother Jones* and a 1995 profile in *Vanity Fair* included interviews with former staffers and neighbors who claimed that Gingrich had repeated affairs while he was married to Jackie and while running for Congress.[223]

According to *Mother Jones*:

"Another former friend maintains that Gingrich repeatedly made sexual advances to her when her husband was out of

town. *On one occasion, he visited under the guise of comforting her after the death of a relative, and instead tried to seduce her. In certain circles in the mid-1970s, Gingrich was developing a reputation as a ladies' man.*"[224]

Dot Crews, Gingrich's campaign scheduler, claimed that it was "common knowledge" that Gingrich had affairs:

"It was common knowledge that Newt was involved with other women during his marriage to Jackie. Maybe not on the level of John Kennedy. But he had girlfriends—some serious, some trivial."[225]

Carter claimed that Gingrich's affair negatively impacted the 1974 campaign:

"We'd have won in 1974 if we could have kept him out of the office, screwing her on the desk."[226]

Carter also recounted having Gingrich's two young daughters with him when he saw Gingrich having oral sex in a parked car:

"As I got to the car, I saw Newt in the passenger seat and one of the guys' wives with her head in his lap going up and down. Newt kind of turned and gave me his little-boy smile. Fortunately Jackie Sue and Kathy were a lot younger and shorter then."[227]

Gingrich Consistently Refused to Address Specific Allegations, Instead Admitted to Sin

In 1984, in response to allegations of infidelity in his first marriage, Gingrich told *Mother Jones*:

"I'm not going to get into those details or the questions about 1974. I think there is a level of personal life that is personal. . . . I had married my high-school math teacher two days after I was 19. In some ways it was a wonderful relationship, particularly in the early years. . . . But we had

*gone through a series of problems—which I regard, I think
legitimately, as private—but which were real. There was an
11-year history prior to my finally breaking down, and short
of someone writing a psychological biography of me, I don't
think it's relevant."*[228]

Gingrich told the reporter that he felt his actions were "inconsistent" with his public statements on family values and that
he altered his rhetoric to address this concern:

*"In fact I think they were sufficiently inconsistent that at one
point in 1979 and 1980, I began to quit saying them in
public. One of the reasons I ended up getting a divorce was
that if I was disintegrating enough as a person that I could
not say those things, then I needed to get my life straight, not
quit saying them. And I think that literally was the crisis I
came to. I guess I look back on it a little bit like somebody
who's in Alcoholics Anonymous—it was a very, very bad
period of my life, and it had been getting steadily worse. . . . I
ultimately wound up at a point where probably suicide or going insane or divorce were the last three options."*[229]

Gingrich has admitted to being a "sinner":

*"I would say to you unequivocally—it will probably sound
pious and sanctimonious saying it—I am a sinner. I am a
normal person. I am like everyone else I ever met. One of
the reasons I go to God is that I ain't very good—I'm not
perfect."*[230]

On another occasion, he told the *Washington Post* that he
had led a "human life":

*"I start with an assumption that all human beings sin and
that all human beings are in fact human. I assume that all
reporters fit the same category. And I think one of the things
that increases our cynicism is creating a totally phony model
that says you're either a total saint or you can't speak, which
is crazy. So all I'll say is that I've led a human life."*[231]

101

Woman Claims that in Affair with Gingrich, Only Had Oral Sex to Ensure Deniability

In September 1995, *Vanity Fair* published an article in which Anne Manning, a former Gingrich campaign volunteer, claimed that she had a months-long affair with Gingrich while he was married to Jackie. It was the first time that Manning had spoken about the affair, and it received widespread news coverage. According to Manning, Gingrich would only have oral sex so that he could deny the sexual relationship:

> *"We had oral sex. He prefers that modus operandi because then he can say, 'I never slept with her.'"*[232]

Manning called Gingrich "morally dishonest" and claimed he threatened to accuse her of lying if she revealed their relationship:

> *Indeed, before Gingrich left that evening, she says, he threatened her: "If you ever tell anybody about this, I'll say you're lying."*[233]

Did Not Directly Deny Charges, but Suggested Accusations Were a Left-Wing Conspiracy

In a radio interview following the publication of the *Vanity Fair* article with Manning's allegations, Gingrich did not deny the affair but instead suggested that liberals were trying to derail his agenda:

> *"I knew when we started down this road . . . if we're going to have a revolution to replace the welfare state, we better expect those people who love it to throw the kitchen sink at us. And they have thrown the kitchen sink and other parts of the house as well."*[234]

Gingrich refused to comment specifically on the allegations, instead branding the article "tabloid journalism":

"I'm not going to comment. That's the kind of tabloid journalism that goes with the territory. We're trying to focus on things that matter to the American people, and we're not going to get involved in that kind of gossip. We're not going to comment, period."[235]

Gingrich's aide, Tony Blankley, echoed his boss's sentiments:

"It's trash and I don't see any reason to get into hateful allegations from hateful people from 20 years ago. It's just a bunch of tabloid psychobabble."[236]

Married Second Wife Six Months after Divorce Finalized, Admitted to Six-Year Affair During Second Divorce

In 1981, Gingrich married Marianne Ginther, whom he met at a political fund-raiser.[237]

In 1999, Gingrich reportedly asked Marianne for a divorce over the phone while she was visiting her mother. Marianne has said that she was "blindsided" by the request. The divorce played out in the papers until the Gingriches finally settled in mediation in December 1999.[238]

Prior to the settlement, Marianne had asked Gingrich to provide the following information:

"The names of anyone else he's slept with during the marriage, with dates and times.

"A list of money or property he's given or lent to any other sexual partners.

"His thoughts on whether he has behaved according to the concept of 'family values' he espoused.

"Examples of conduct that either partner committed that contributed to their separation."[239]

Third Wife Subpoenaed During Second Divorce Trial, but Claimed Could Not Testify Because Adultery Illegal in D.C.

As early as 1995, Gingrich had a relationship with his third wife, Callista Bisek. According to *Vanity Fair*:

"Since Newt became a national celebrity, he has no shortage of female admirers—from Callista Bisek, a former aide in Congressman Steve Gunderson's office who has been a favorite breakfast companion."[240]

During his 1999 divorce from Ginther, Gingrich admitted to a six-year affair with Bisek, who ultimately became his third wife. As he had with Marianne, Gingrich met Bisek at a fundraiser. Bisek was 33 years old at the time and worked for the House Agriculture Committee.[241]

During the divorce, Ginther attempted to compel Bisek to appear for a videotaped deposition. Bisek argued that she could not be required to testify because of "the constitutional prohibition against self-incrimination because adultery is a crime in the District of Columbia."[242]

Had Second Marriage Annulled After Marrying Third Wife, Ultimately Renewed Vows in Catholic Ceremony

Gingrich and Bisek were married in August 2000. In 2002, Gingrich asked the archdioceses of Atlanta to annul his marriage to Ginther, despite the fact that their marriage was Lutheran, not Catholic.[243]

In August 2003, after receiving the annulment, Gingrich and Bisek renewed their vows in a Catholic ceremony.[244]

Mom Said Third Marriage "First Time" She Believed "Newty Is in Love"

According to Gingrich's mother, Kit, his marriage to Bisek is his most successful:

"I liked her from the first time I saw her. This is the first time I can ever remember seeing that Newty is in love. When you see him, he just beams."[245]

Did Not Criticize Clinton for Adultery, Instead Focused on Lying under Oath

In 1998, Gingrich told the *Washington Post* that Clinton should be impeached because of "a pattern of felonies" and "not a single human mistake." Gingrich said the Lewinsky situation was not sufficient for impeachment:

"I don't think the Congress could move forward only on Lewinsky."[246]

Admitted to Extramarital Affair During Lewinsky Scandal, Claimed Situation Different Because Did Not Lie Under Oath

In 2007, Gingrich admitted in an interview with Reverend James Dobson that he was involved in an extramarital affair at the same time that Clinton was involved with Monica Lewinsky. Gingrich distinguished himself from Clinton by noting that he never lied under oath:

"I had been through a divorce, I had been through depositions. If you don't tell the truth under oath, the whole system breaks down."[247]

GIRLFRIEND, FIRST

(see **Mule**)

GOMORRAH, SLOUCHING TOWARD

(see **All of the Above and Below**)

GROPING

FORMER HAWAII HOUSE MINORITY LEADER CHARGED WITH ABUSIVE SEXUAL CONDUCT AFTER GROPING A SLEEPING STRANGER ON AN AIRPLANE

In December 2004, Hawaii legislator Galen Fox was arrested for groping the woman seated next to him on a flight from Honolulu to Los Angeles. The 27-year-old woman had taken a Dramamine and fallen asleep. When she awoke, she felt a "warm sensation against her crotch and discovered the male passenger in the seat next to her . . . had his hands in her jeans and was rubbing her crotch."[248]

Fox explained that he thought the sleeping woman's lack of response after he rubbed against her arm and leg signaled that she was "interested in some physical contact."[249]

After his arrest, Fox issued a statement: "I vigorously fought charges against me, which I hold to be untrue."[250]

In court, however, he admitted that he intentionally rubbed her crotch and that "she did not invite his conduct nor give him permission to touch her."

The judge in the case read a letter from the victim: "Since that flight, I have had difficulty sleeping and I have been having nightmares of Galen Fox... I brought this case because I had the right to sleep on a plane without being groped."[251]

Fox was charged with abusive sexual conduct, sentenced to three months of house arrest and three years' probation, and ordered to seek psychiatric treatment. [252]

REPUBLICAN GOVERNOR ACCUSED OF GROPING AND SEXUAL HARASSMENT BY MULTIPLE WOMEN

In October 2003, during the California recall election, the *Los Angeles Times* wrote a story about six women who accused then-candidate Arnold Schwarzenegger of fondling and sexually harassing them. Four of the women said that he groped them, another charged that he tried to take off her swimsuit, and still another claimed that he had pulled her onto his lap and asked her about a particular sex act. [253]

Although Schwarzenegger denied remembering any of the incidents and called the story "trash politics," he offered a broad apology to the women:

"I always say that wherever there is smoke, there is fire.

"So I want to say to you, yes, I have behaved badly sometimes. Yes, it is true that I was on rowdy movie sets, and I have done things that were not right, which I thought then was playful. But I now recognize that I have offended people. And to those people that I have offended, I want to say to them, I am deeply sorry about that, and I apologize." [254]

Admitted to Orgies with Other Bodybuilders at His Gym

In an interview in the adult magazine *Oui*, the future governor discussed partaking in group sex with fellow bodybuilders at his gym:

"Everyone jumped on [the woman] and took her upstairs where we all got together."

"Where there is smoke, there is fire."
—*Governor Arnold Schwarzenegger*

Not all the bodybuilders participated, he added, "just the guys who can fuck in front of other guys. Not everybody can do that. Some think that they don't have a big-enough cock, so they can't get a hard-on."[255]

GROPING OF LAW ENFORCEMENT OFFICIALS

HEAD OF CONSERVATIVE LEGAL FOUNDATION THAT SOUGHT CLINTON'S DISBARMENT AND SUPPORTED OTHER CONSERVATIVE LEGAL ACTIONS PLEADS GUILTY TO INDECENCY IN NATIONAL PARK

In May 2000, Matthew J. Glavin was arrested for indecency in the Chattahoochee River National Recreation Area after he masturbated in front of and grabbed the groin of a male park ranger. Glavin initially denied the charges but ultimately pleaded guilty.[256]

In December 2000, Glavin was fined $1,000, sentenced to one year probation, and banned from federal parks during the probation. The judge rejected the prosecutor's request for three months house arrest, saying it would interfere with Glavin's alcohol treatment program.[257]

After he was arrested, it was revealed that Glavin had pleaded guilty to a similar charge in 1996, paid a $1,000 fine, and served six months probation.[258]

At the time of his arrest, Glavin had headed the conservative Southeastern Legal Foundation for six years. The foundation was seeking President Clinton's disbarment and had submitted briefs in support of the Boy Scouts' effort to ban gay Scout leaders and in support of anti-affirmative action litigation.[259]

UTAH STATE LEGISLATOR RESIGNS AFTER ARREST FOR SOLICITING MALE PROSTITUTE, PLEADS GUILTY TO CHARGE

In March 2003, Utah State Representative Brent Parker (R-Wellsville) resigned after he was arrested in Salt Lake City for soliciting an undercover male police officer for sex. According to the arrest report, Parker grabbed the police officer's crotch, offered him $20, and asked for his number so he could call him whenever he was in town. Parker was married at the time with grown children and grandchildren.[260]

Three days after his arrest, reporters with Salt Lake City *Deseret News* approached Parker on the floor of the state house to get his reaction to the charges. He begged them to hold the story until the end of the legislative session, but they refused. Parker handed House Speaker Marty Stephens a handwritten resignation letter, effective immediately, and fled the building.[261]

In April 2003, Parker pleaded guilty to soliciting sex. The court agreed to drop the charge against Parker in a year if he completed a ten-week "Johns Program" designed to treat sex solicitors. Parker's wife stood by him as he apologized to family and friends:

> *"I apologize to my family, church, community and constituents."*[262]

*"And Guys, if you exploit a girl,
it will come back to get you.
That's called 'Karma.'"* [263]

—BILL O'REILLY, Conservative Commentator,
in his book *The O'Reilly Factor for Kids*

HARASSMENT, SEXUAL

CONSERVATIVE TALK SHOW HOST SETTLES SEXUAL HARASSMENT SUIT

In October 2004, conservative talk-show host Bill O'Reilly settled a sexual harassment suit brought against him by a female producer of his show. Andrea Mackris claimed that O'Reilly repeatedly spoke to her "about sexual fantasies, masturbation and vibrators while sometimes seeming to pleasure himself." In one oft-reported fantasy, O'Reilly described rubbing Mackris' privates with a falafel (confusing the Middle Eastern staple for a loofah).[264]

In addition, Mackris claimed that O'Reilly propositioned her and a female friend. O'Reilly was not required to apologize or admit guilt under the settlement.[265]

After the settlement, O'Reilly told his viewers that there was "no wrongdoing in the case whatsoever by anyone."[266]

Mackris alleged in the suit that O'Reilly threatened her if she went public with the harassment. According to Mackris, O'Reilly said:

> *"If any woman ever breathed a word I'll make her pay so dearly that she'll wish she'd never been born. . . . It'd be her word against mine and who are they going to believe? Me or some unstable woman making outrageous accusations. They'd see her as some psycho, someone unstable."*[267]

It was widely suspected that Mackris had made recordings of her conversations with O'Reilly, as she claimed to have concrete proof and her lawsuit included details of the two's conversations.[268]

*"And then I would take the other hand with the falafel
thing and put it on your . . ."*
—Bill O'Reilly

U.S. SENATOR FORCED TO RESIGN AFTER WOMEN ALLEGES SEXUAL HARASSMENT, DIARIES REVEAL POSSIBLE CRIMINAL BEHAVIOR

In October 1995, U.S. Senator Bob Packwood (R-OR) resigned after a 33-month investigation revealed that he sexually harassed multiple staff members and other women and that he used his office to try to obtain a job for his ex-wife. The Senate Ethics Committee recommended his expulsion. Packwood had written about his sexual escapades in his diaries, though he altered the diaries after being forced to turn them over to Senate investigators.[269]

According to the *Washington Post*, the diaries included the following entries:

> *In one diary entry he reflects that it his "Christian duty" to have sex with one woman who was not getting any: "She's got this little body, and she had about five glasses of wine."* [269a]

At one point Packwood refers to "the 22 staff members I'd made love to and probably 75 others I've had a passionate relationship with."[270]

SUPREME COURT JUSTICE ACCUSED DURING SENATE CONFIRMATION OF SEXUAL HARASSMENT BY A FORMER SUBORDINATE

When the first President Bush nominated Judge Clarence Thomas to the Supreme Court, many criticized the decision, claiming that the nominee was ideologically outside the mainstream and lacked the necessary qualifications. Indeed, Thomas had been given the lowest rating from the American Bar Association of any high court nominee since 1955.[271]

What held up the confirmation hearings, however, wasn't Thomas' views of affirmative action or *Roe vs. Wade*. The proceedings garnered a tremendous amount of public attention due to debates about zoological pornography, an adult star by the name of Long Dong Silver, and a strand of pubic hair on a Coke can.

Anita Hill, who had worked for Thomas at the Department of Education, testified before the U.S. Senate that the nominee had sexually harassed her:

> *"On several occasions," Hill testified under oath, "Thomas told me graphically of his own sexual prowess. . . . My efforts to change the subject were rarely successful."*[272]

He pressured her to see him socially, she said, trying to entice her with descriptions of the size of his penis and his prowess at oral sex. Hill testified that Thomas was obsessed with pornography:

> *"He spoke about acts he had seen in pornographic films involving such matters as women having sex with animals, and films showing group sex or rape scenes. He talked about pornographic materials depicting individuals with large penises, or large breasts in various sex acts."*[273]

Hill described one incident in which Thomas accused his colleagues of placing a pubic hair on his can of soda:

> *"One of the oddest episodes I remember was an occasion in which Thomas was drinking a Coke in his office, he got up from the table at which we were working, went over to his desk to get the Coke, looked at the can and asked, 'Who has put pubic hair on my Coke?"*[274]

A friend in college claimed that he remembered Thomas pulling a similar stunt.[275]

Hill passed a lie detector test but Thomas, who refuted all her allegations of inappropriate behavior, refused to take one. However, in the end, the Senate confirmed Thomas 52-48—the narrowest margin of victory for a Supreme Court nominee in over a century.[276]

VIRGINIA HOUSE SPEAKER FORCED TO RESIGN IN WAKE OF SEXUAL HARASSMENT ALLEGATIONS

In July 2002, S.Vance Wilkins, the speaker of the Virginia House, resigned his speakership and his position after it was revealed that he paid $100,000 to settle a sexual harassment suit. The *Washington Post* reported in June 2002 that Wilkins paid the 26-year-old woman $100,000 after she claimed that he repeatedly made advances toward her while she worked at the offices of a construction company he once owned.[277]

The *Richmond Times Dispatch* reported that, at the time of his resignation, Wilkins "said he had engaged in friendly behavior with women that was acceptable in another era."[278]

In December 2002, the *Richmond Times Dispatch* reported that S. Vance Wilkins, Jr., and his wife of 20 years, Leona, had separated and planned to divorce. Six months earlier, Leona stood by her husband's side when he announced his resignation from the Virginia House after it was revealed that he paid $100,000 to settle a sexual harassment lawsuit brought against him.[279]

SEE ALSO:

Governor Arnold Schwarzenegger (R-CA) **(Groping)**

HILLARY DUFF

DA Mark Pazuhanich (see **Fondling**)

HOSPITAL VISIT

U.S. Representative Newt Gingrich (R-GA) (see **Gingrich Family Values**)

HOTMILITARYSTUD.COM

Jeff Gannon, a.k.a. James Dale Guckert, Conservative Commentator (see **Escort**)

HYPERSEXUALITY

U.S. Representative Joe McDade (R-PA) (see **Indecent Exposure**)

HYPOCRISY

(see **All of Above and Below**)

*"It was my own private life,
and I don't consider myself a public figure."*[280]

—SUSAN CARPENTER McMILLAN, Anti-Abortion Activist

IMPEACHMENT, ADVOCATES OF CLINTON'S

CONTROVERSIAL EX-GEORGIA CONGRESSMAN MARRIED THREE TIMES, LICKS WHIPPED CREAM OFF WOMEN'S BREASTS AT CHARITY EVENT

Former Republican Congressman Bob Barr (GA) has been married three times and was a leader of the impeachment proceedings against President Clinton. Barr's marital troubles were an issue in his 1994 campaign, including a dispute with his second wife over medical expenses.[281]

In 1998, *Slate* reported that Barr had been sued for child support.[282]

An oft-reported incident involving Barr at a benefit for the Leukemia Society occurred before he was elected to Congress. Barr's tablemates paid $200 to the charity for Barr to lick whipped cream off two "buxom" women.[283] When asked in 1998, if he would have licked the women if he had it to do over again, Barr said no:

> *"Heavens no! It was a charity event . . . and people were having a good time."* [284]

In 1999, *Hustler* founder Larry Flynt held a press conference to reveal that Barr, who had previously equated abortion to murder on the House floor, had, in 1983, "acquiesced to his then-wife having an abortion." In 1985, Flynt revealed, Barr had invoked legal privilege to refuse answering questions about whether he had cheated on his second wife with the woman who would become his third.[285]

*When asked in '98 if he would have licked the women over again,
Barr responded, "Heavens no!"*

REPUBLICAN CONGRESSMAN LEADING CLINTON IMPEACHMENT TRIAL ADMITTED TO EXTRAMARITAL AFFAIRS IN 1960s

In 1998, *Salon* revealed that U.S. Congressman Henry Hyde (R-IL) had a six-year-long extramarital affair with Cherie Soskin in the 1960s. Both Hyde and Soskin were married with small children at the time and Hyde was serving in the Illinois legislature.[286]

Hyde referred to the affair as a "long, long time ago":

"The statute of limitations has long since passed on my youthful indiscretions. Suffice it to say, Cherie [Soskin] and I were good friends a long, long time ago. After [her husband] confronted my wife, the friendship ended and my marriage remained intact."[287]

After Hyde responded to the story, Soskin's daughter claimed that her mother was offended by Hyde's downplaying of their relationship and that the affair continued after Hyde's wife learned of it. She also claimed that her mother said she knew of other adulterous affairs by Hyde.[288]

"My mother originally didn't want me to say anything to the press, but she's just so fed up with [Hyde], with how two-faced he is. She knows she wasn't his first [mistress] and she wasn't his last. She hates his anti-abortion stuff, and all the family values stuff. She thinks he's bad for the country, he's too powerful and he's hypocritical."[289]

SEE ALSO:

U.S. Representative Dan Burton (R-IN) **(Adultery)**

U.S. Representative Helen Chenoweth (R-ID) **(Adultery)**

Richard Delgaudio, Conservative Fund-Raiser **(Child Pornography)**

U.S. Representative Newt Gingrich (R-GA) **(Gingrich Family Values)**

Marty Glickman, Conservative Commentator (**Unlawful Sexual Activity**)

INCEST

REPUBLICAN CANDIDATE FOR NEVADA ASSEMBLY PLEADS GUILTY TO MOLESTING DAUGHTERS

In 2004, Richard Gardner, Jr., ran as a Republican in the Nevada Assembly District 14 race despite the fact that he had pleaded guilty to molesting his daughters in California in 1988.[290]

Gardner called his behavior a "terrible mistake" but said he had paid his debt to society:

> *"When a person pays what a society demands from them for a crime they committed, it's paid for."*[291]

COUNTY REPUBLICAN PARTY CHAIR SPENT 14 YEARS IN PRISON FOR RAPING DAUGHTERS

In 1988, Paul Ingram was arrested and charged with molesting two women and performing satanic rituals with them. Ingram ultimately confessed to raping his daughters and spent 14 years in prison for his crimes. Ingram later claimed that he was innocent and that he was brainwashed by authorities into giving the confession.[292]

At the time of his arrest, Ingram was the fourth highest ranking officer in the Thurston County, Washington, sheriff's department and was the immediate past chairman of the Thurston County Republican Party.[293]

State Representative Larry Jack Schwarz (R-CO)
(Pornography)

INCREDIBLY BENEVOLENT

Richard A. Dasen, Sr., Conservative Activist (see **Rape**)

INDECENT EXPOSURE

CONSERVATIVE TALK SHOW HOST CONVICTED OF EXPOSING GENITALS TO 11-YEAR-OLD GIRL

In November 2003, Houston conservative radio talk show host and critic of President Clinton's personal life Jon Matthews was arrested and charged with exposing his genitals to an 11-year-old girl who lived in his neighborhood. Matthews denied the charge but pleaded guilty to indecency with a child in June 2004 in exchange for deferred adjudication, which allowed him to avoid jail time.[294]

Dan Patrick, now a Texas state representative and the owner of the radio station where Matthews worked, said that he was praying for Matthews:

"The law has worked through its course. Justice apparently has been done. I pray for the victim and I pray for Jon."[295]

In August 2006, Matthews was arrested for violating the terms of his deferred adjudication agreement, including abusing alcohol and engaging in sexual fantasy over the Internet involving a three-year-old boy. Matthews faced up to ten years

123

in prison (the maximum sentence on his original charge) for violating the agreement.[296]

EX-CONGRESSMAN ACCUSED OF EXPOSURE AT FLORIDA RESORT

In February 2007, at least three guests at a Sanibel, Florida, resort reported that former Congressman Joe McDade (R-PA) fondled himself while standing by the hotel pool. The police responded to a 911 call alleging the indecent exposure. McDade served in the U.S. House of Representatives from 1963 to 1999 and chose to retire after being diagnosed with Parkinson's disease.[297]

McDade entered a written plea of not guilty to the charge on May 1, 2007.[298]

Doctor Told Newspaper Behavior Could Be Attributable to Parkinson's Drugs

In February 2007, Dr. Melissa J. Nirenberg of the Cornell Medical Center told the *Times Leader* that McDade's behavior could be attributable to some Parkinson's drugs that are "linked to hypersexuality and impulse-control disorders."[299]

TENNESSEE STATE LEGISLATOR COMMITTED SUICIDE AFTER ARRESTED AND CHARGED WITH SEVEN COUNTS OF LEWD EXPOSURE TO MINORS

In June 2002, Tennessee State Representative Keith Westmoreland (R-Kingsport) was arrested at the Hilton Hotel in Sandestin, Florida, on seven counts of lewd and lascivious exhibition to minors. Westmoreland was accused of exposing his genitals at the hotel pool and hot tub. Westmoreland committed suicide three days after his arrest was reported in the news.[300]

After Westmoreland's arrest was reported, the Nashville police revealed that Westmoreland was twice questioned in March 2002 for exposing himself to minors at two different Nashville hotels. Westmoreland was not charged following either incident.[301]

SEE ALSO:

Matthew J. Glavin, Head of the Southeastern Legal Foundation (**Groping of Law Enforcement Officials**)

INGRATITUDE

U.S. Representative Newt Gingrich (R–GA) (see **Gingrich Family Values**)

INFIDELITY

(see **Adultery**)

INSTANT MESSAGES

U.S. Representative Mark Foley (R–FL) (see **Pages, Congressional**)

Jon Matthews, Conservative Commentator (see **Indecent Exposure**)

INTENSELY PERSONAL RELATIONSHIP

U.S. Representative Bill Thomas (R–CA) (see **Adultery**)

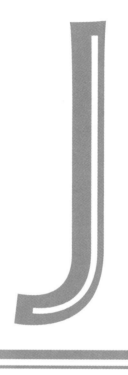

"Our founding fathers knew that political leaders' personal conduct must be held to the highest standard." [302]

—Representative HELEN CHENOWETH (R-ID)

JOHNS PROGRAM

State Representative Brent Parker (R-UT) (see **Groping of Law Enforcement Officials**)

JUDGMENT, BAD

(see **All of Above and Below**)

"The Bible says that people should love each other and show affection." [303]

—Pastor ROBERT GRAY, to a young girl he sexually abused, according to the lawsuit against him

KIDDIE PORN

(see **Child Pornography**)

KISSING

Pastor Robert Gray (see **Battery, Sexual**)

"*They (Victorians) reduced the number of children born out of wedlock by almost 50 per cent. They changed the whole momentum of their society. They didn't do it through a new bureaucracy, but by re-establishing values, by moral leadership and by being willing to look at people in the face and say, 'You should be ashamed when you get drunk in public. You ought to be ashamed if you're a drug addict'.*"[304]

—Representative NEWT GINGRICH (R-GA)

LITTLE-BOY SMILE

U.S. Representative Newt Gingrich (R-GA) (see **Gingrich Family Values**)

LOBBYIST

CONGRESSMAN CARRIED ON AFFAIR WITH LOBBYIST INVOLVED WITH HIS COMMITTEE

In 2003, Stephen LaTourette (R-OH) phoned his wife of 21 years to let her know he wanted a divorce. The Republican congressman from Ohio's 14th District had helped lead the charge for President Clinton's impeachment and voted for it, despite the fact that he was having an affair at the time with his former chief of staff, who happened to be a lobbyist for a firm pushing legislation before the House Transportation and Infrastructure Committee—a committee on which the congressman served.[305]

In 2004, when LaTourette ran for re-election in the midst of controversy over charges that he had tried to do favors for disgraced lobbyist Jack Abramoff, his by-then former wife planted his opponent's yard sign in her yard.

"My congressperson should be honest, truthful and decent, and she exemplifies those qualities," she explained.[306]

*"I am not gay,
I don't do these kinds of things."*[307]

—Senator LARRY CRAIG (R-ID)

MEN'S ROOMS

FLORIDA REPRESENTATIVE ARRESTED FOR OFFERING MALE UNDERCOVER COP $20 TO PERFORM ORAL SEX

In July 2007, Florida State Representative Bob Allen was arrested for soliciting oral sex from an undercover cop. Allen was stripped of his committee assignments after the arrest was revealed and stepped down as co-chair of John McCain's Florida presidential campaign.[308]

Allen claimed that he was not soliciting sex and that he was only "playing along" because he was afraid the African American police officer would harm him. In his statement to police, Allen said he "was about to be a statistic" and that he would have said anything to get away:

> *"I certainly wasn't there to have sex with anybody and certainly wasn't there to exchange money for it.*
>
> *"This was a pretty stocky black guy, and there was nothing but other black guys around in the park."*[309]

According to the *Orlando Sentinel*, the police reported that Allen was acting suspiciously and recorded the following events:

> *After peering over the stall a second time, Allen pushed open the door and joined Kavanaugh inside, the officer wrote. Allen muttered "hi," and then said, "this is kind of a public place, isn't it," the report said.* [309a]

"Well look, man, I'm trying to make some money; you think you can hook me up with 20 bucks?" Kavanaugh asked Allen.

The officer said Allen responded, "Sure, I can do that, but this place is too public."

Then Kavanaugh said he told Allen, "I wanna know what I gotta do for 20 bucks before we leave." He said Allen replied: "I don't know what you're into."

According to Kavanaugh's statement, the officer said, "do you want just [oral sex]?" and Allen replied, "I was thinking you would want one."

The officer said he then asked Allen, "but you'll still give me the 20 bucks for that." . . . and that the legislator said, "yeah, I wouldn't argue with that."[310]

The arresting officers reported that Allen asked if it would help him if he told them he was a state legislator. Allen claimed he was only telling them that before they saw his official license plates:

> *"I don't know if it makes any difference, but once you get to the car you will see I'm a state legislator."* [310a]

As a member of the Florida House, Allen had sponsored the Lewd or Lascivious Exhibition Act—a bill that would increase penalties for public masturbation in the presence of a consenting adult. The bill failed.[311]

IDAHO SENATOR ARRESTED FOR SOLICITING SEX IN MEN'S BATHROOM

In June 2007, U.S. Senator Larry Craig (R-ID) was arrested by an undercover officer at the Minneapolis airport and charged with lewd behavior. The officer claimed that Craig tapped his foot, touched the officer's foot, and put his hand into the officer's stall—all signs of sex solicitation. When Craig ran his left hand under the stall, the officer could see the senator's gold wedding band. In due course, the man put his own hand under the stall and showed Craig his badge. Craig pleaded guilty to lesser misdemeanor disorderly conduct charges in August 2007, claiming he hoped it would "go away." Instead, *Roll Call* ran the arrest story.[312]

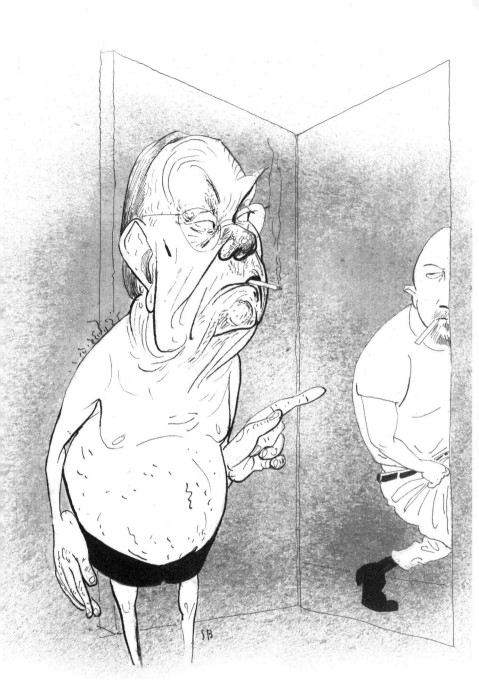

"Just remember, you've never been here, you don't know me."
—Senator Larry Craig

Craig issued a statement denying that he was attempting to solicit sex and expressing regret for pleading guilty to the lesser charge:

> *"At the time of this incident, I complained to the police that they were misconstruing my actions. I was not involved in any inappropriate conduct. I should have had the advice of counsel in resolving this matter. In hindsight, I should not have pled guilty. I was trying to handle this matter myself quickly and expeditiously."*[313]

The arresting officer reported that Craig told him he was a U.S. senator and said "What do you think of that?" The officer also noted that he felt Craig was not being honest about his actions in the bathroom in his post-arrest interview. In the interview, Craig said:

> *"I am not gay; I don't do these kinds of things."*

> *"Your foot came toward mine, mine came towards yours. Was that natural? Did we bump? Yes, I think we did. You said so. I won't dispute that."*[314]

Although Craig initially said that he would resign his Senate seat, he later added the caveat that he would remain in the Senate if he were successful in withdrawing his guilty plea. After a judge denied his petition to withdraw the plea, Craig said he would remain in the Senate and would appeal the judge's decision.[315]

Craig has said that he must remain in the Senate in order to clear his name:

> *"As I continued to work for Idaho over the past three weeks here in the Senate, I have seen that it is possible for me to work here effectively. I will continue my effort to clear my name in the Senate Ethics Committee—something that is not possible if I am not serving in the Senate."*[316]

After Arrest Revealed, Newspaper Publishes Report on Investigation that Contains Several Allegations from Men that Craig Hit on Them, Craig Denies Allegations, Blames Liberals

Two months later, the *Idaho Statesman* detailed a five-month-long investigation of allegations that the senator was a homosexual. Again, Craig insisted that he had never engaged in gay sex, despite several men who came forward to dispute his claims. A "professional man" with "close ties to Republican officials" said he had had oral sex with Craig in 2004 at Washington, D.C.'s, Union Station.[317] Another alleged that Craig had "cruised" him for sex at a Boise REI store. The senator denied these accusations, too:

"Once again, I'm not gay, and I don't cruise, and I don't hit on men. I have no idea how he drew that conclusion. A smile? Here is one thing I do out in public: I make eye contact, I smile at people, they recognize me, they say, 'Oh, hi, Senator.' Or, 'Do I know you?'"

"I've been in this business 27 years in the public eye here. I don't go around anywhere hitting on men, and by God, if I did, I wouldn't do it in Boise, Idaho! Jiminy!"

"The gay movement, we know it for what it is. It's now aggressive and it's liberal and it's naming people to try to put them in compromising, difficult situations."[318]

More accusations surfaced as Craig's anti-gay comments prompted others to come forward. In December, the *Idaho Statesman* revealed that eight additional men were alleging relationships with the senator, one of whom was gay escort Mike Jones, the prostitute who figured in Reverend Ted Haggard's fall from grace.

Jones claimed that Craig paid him $200 for sex in late 2004 or early 2005. He said he went on record after recognizing the senator on TV but had figured him for a closeted politician even during the encounter, which he described in an interview with Craig's hometown newspaper:

> *"He did something that only a few people did that saw me through the years. . . . he kept his clothes on. . . . he took his dress shirt off, and had a T-shirt on, and he undid his zipper, and pulled his penis out, and performed oral sex on me. . . . He was stroking [his penis] as he was performing oral sex on me. . . . My penis was clearly in his mouth. . . . that probably went on for about 20 minutes. Now, the only way I knew that he reached his moment was his moaning and groaning. I just assumed he had reached orgasm, and then he wanted my penis out of his mouth."*[319]

David Phillips, a 42-year-old information technology consultant, claimed that Craig picked him up at a gay club in 1986. The senator led him down an alley to a house and kept reminding him that the sex would be anonymous. "Just remember, you've never been here," Craig warned him. "You don't know me."

Phillips described a similar encounter to the one Jones talked about. The senator brought out condoms and lubricant, and he kept his pants on the whole time they performed fellatio on each other:

> *"He wanted for me to offer him anal sex—for me to receive him," Phillips related. "I did, and he again commented, 'Just remember, you don't know me.'. . . The mess that was created, he was absolutely frantic about, and he didn't want me going into the bathroom to clean myself up. He just wanted me to put my clothes back on and leave. I just had never been treated that way by a man before."*[320]

According to Phillips, Craig hurried him out of the house, put $20 in his pocket, and said, "Remember, you haven't been here. Just remember, I could buy and sell your ass a thousand times over."

Phillips claimed that he "drove home in probably an hour and half of traffic in soiled underwear and feeling totally humiliated. I didn't hear that voice again until the end of August, when this all just came back to me."[321]

In 1982, Preemptively Denied Having Sex with Male Pages During House Page Scandal

In 1982, former House page Leroy Williams told CBS News that he had sex with three House members when he was 17 years old. Williams later recanted his story. Williams did not name the House members. Craig preemptively issued a statement claiming that newspapers had contacted him and threatened to name him as one of the three members and denying that he had sex with the page. The two newspapers he cited denied that they planned to name him. Craig claimed the allegations were "part of a concerted effort at character assassination" and denied having sex with male pages:

> *"I have done nothing that I need to be either publicly or privately ashamed of. I am guilty of no crime or impropriety, and I am convinced that this is an effort to damage my personal character and destroy my political career."*[322]

In addition, Craig voluntarily went to the FBI to be interviewed about the allegations and took a polygraph test. In his interview with the FBI, Craig claimed he had never had homosexual relations.[323]

LOUISIANA COUNCILMEMBER TWICE STOPPED FOR SUSPECTED LEWD BEHAVIOR IN MEN'S ROOMS, FORCED TO WITHDRAW FROM STATE SENATE RACE AFTER RECORD REVEALED

In October 2007, St. Bernard Parish Councilman Joey DiFatta resigned from his race for the Louisiana Senate after it was revealed that he had twice been detained by police for lewd behavior in public restrooms since 1996.[324]

DiFatta denied that he had done anything wrong and noted that he was not convicted on either count:

"If I had done something wrong, I would have been arrested. I was not. I will deny that I was involved in any activity of that nature."[325]

In 1996, Kenner, Louisiana, police issued a misdemeanor summons for DiFatta in connection with an incident in a mall restroom in which a man claimed that DiFatta peeked at him through a hole in a bathroom stall. The complainant ultimately dropped the charges.[326]

In 2000, Jefferson Parish deputy's working undercover in a mall restroom detained DiFatta after they said he signaled with his foot that he wanted to engage in sexual activity and reached under a stall to rub the leg of an undercover deputy. According to the report, the deputy asked DiFatta, "What do you want?" and DiFatta responded, "I want to play with you." DiFatta was not arrested because children entered the bathroom and the deputy terminated the interview. The deputy claimed that he confronted DiFatta, who promised not to return to the restroom and said that he had "a problem with such behavior and had sought counseling for the addiction in the past."[327]

SEE ALSO:

Committeeman Andrew Buhr (Hadley Township, MO)
(Sodomy, Statutory)

METHAMPHETAMINES

(see **Drugs**)

MONOGAMY, SERIAL

U.S. Representative Bob Barr (R-GA) (see **Impeachment, Advocate of Clinton's**)

MULE

Neal Horsley, Anti-Gay/Anti-Abortion Crusader
(see **Bestiality**)

"I don't believe there's any issue that's more important than this one."[328]

—Senator DAVID VITTER (R-LA),
on a constitutional amendment banning same-sex marriage
to "protect the sanctity of traditional marriages"

NARCOLEPTIC SEX

Dr. W. David Hager, FDA Advisor (see **Sodomy, Nonconsensual**)

NECROPHILIA

(research pending)

NUDE PHOTOS

NUDE PHOTOS OF CONSERVATIVE TALK SHOW HOST POSTED ON INTERNET; OPPOSED TO ADULTERY AND DIVORCE, BUT HAD AFFAIR AND DIVORCED

In 1998, Bill Ballance, an L.A.-based radio talk show host whom Dr. Laura Schlessinger had called a "mentor," sold 23-year-old nude photos of Schlessinger to a Web site, which posted the photos online. That same year, Dr. Laura spoke out against the American Libraries Association for sexual education material that she considered "pornographic."[329]

Schlessinger and Ballance were dating when the photos were taken. Ballance also claimed that he dated Schlessinger while she was still married to her first husband. Schlessinger was famous for her radio talk show in which she counseled against divorce and shamed those who had affairs.[330]

Schlessinger sued to try to force the Web site to remove the photos but lost her suit. In the immediate wake of the photos release, Schlessinger noted that she had long admitted to sin in her past and called Ballance's release of the photos "morally reprehensible":

"It isn't news to my longtime listeners and those who read my books that I have undergone profound changes over the course of my life—the most important of which is my journey from atheist to observant Jew. In my 20s, I was on my own moral authority. The inadequacy of that way of life is painfully obvious now."

"I am mystified as to why, 23 years later, this 80-year-old man would do such a morally reprehensible thing."[331]

In 2000, in an interview with Maria Shriver, Schlessinger said of the uproar surrounding the release of the pictures:

"You'd think I'd spent, you know, 15 years running a bordello. So I have a year and a half after a divorce that I'm sort of clicking my heels a little bit. And suddenly, I'm turned into this harlot. It's hysterical, but it's not accurate."[332]

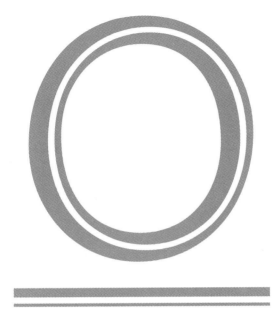

"I'm always gentle and loving;
not to worry;
no damage ever;
no rough stuff ever ever . . .
I've done it plenty."[333]

—JOHN DAVID "ROY" ATCHISON, Republican Federal Prosecutor

OFFICE FURNITURE

U.S. Representative Newt Gingrich (R–GA) (see **Gingrich Family Values**)

ORAL SEX

(see **Blow Jobs**)

ORGIES

Alfred Bloomingdale, Reagan Advisor (see **S&M**)

Rev. Ted Haggard (see **Prostitution**)

Governor Arnold Schwarzenegger (R–CA) (see **Groping**)

"We need to completely change the way
we treat sex offenders. They are not petty
criminals—they prey on children like animals
and will continue to do so unless stopped. . . .
This bill will make prey of predators who
victimize our children."[334]

—Representative MARK FOLEY (R–FL)

PAGES, CONGRESSIONAL

HOUSE OF REPRESENTATIVES VOTES TO CENSURE CONGRESSMAN AFTER HE ADMITS TO HAVING SEX ON SEVERAL OCCASIONS WITH A 17-YEAR-OLD HOUSE PAGE

In 1983, the House voted 289-136 to censure Daniel Crane (R-ID); Crane voted for his own censure. The House also censured Congressman Gerry Studds (D-MA), who admitted to sex with a male page.[335]

Crane apologized to his colleagues before the vote:

"Mr. Speaker, this is one of the most difficult moments in my life and it has been an unparalleled ordeal for my family.

"I have not yet apologized to my colleagues in this body for the shame I have brought down on this institution.

"Before any action is taken, and regardless of the action this body takes, I want the members to know that I am sorry and that I apologize to one and all."[336]

Crane also noted that God would forgive him:

"We pay for our sins in life, and in making my peace I take comfort that our Lord promised me forgiveness 70 times seven."[337]

REPUBLICAN CONGRESSMAN RESIGNS, CHECKS INTO REHAB AFTER REVELATIONS OF SEXUALLY EXPLICIT IMS WITH HOUSE PAGES

In 2006, U.S. Congressman Mark Foley (R-FL) resigned his position and checked himself into a treatment facility for alcoholism and "other behavioral problems," after sexually explicit instant messages between him and male House pages were revealed by the media.[338]

Previously, Foley had dismissed allegations he was gay as "revolting and unforgivable."[339]

Foley's lawyer noted that Foley had been molested as a young teenager by a member of the clergy.[340]

The Foley situation divided the Republican leadership, who accused one another of not doing enough to address the situation with Foley after previous warnings that he was overly friendly with House pages. Some conservatives called for the resignation of House Speaker Dennis Hastert over his handling of the situation.[341]

PASSIONATE RELATIONSHIP

U.S. Senator Bob Packwood (R-OR) (see **Sexual Harassment**)

PEDOPHILIA

Mayor Tom Adams (Green Oaks, IL) (see **Child Pornography**)

Randal David Ankeney, Employee of Governor Bill Owens (see **Assault, Sexual**)

Federal Prosecutor John David "Roy" Atchison (see **Soliciting Sex w/ a Minor**)

County Commissioner Merrill Robert Barter (Lincoln, ME) (see **Child Molestation**)

Parker J. Bena, Virginia Elector (see **Child Pornography**)

Lou Beres, Oregon Christian Coalition Leader (see Child Molestation)

Howard L. Brooks, Legislative Aide (see Child Molestation)

John Allen Burt, Anti-Abortion Crusader (see Child Molestation)

Councilman Keola Childs (Kealakekua, HI) (see Child Molestation)

Kevin Coan, Director of the St. Louis Election Board (see Soliciting Sex w/ a Minor)

Councilman John J. Collins (Eatontown, PA) (see Assault, Sexual)

Carey Lee Cramer, Republican Media Consultant (see Child Molestation)

Richard A. Dasen, Sr., Conservative Activist (see Rape)

Richard Delgaudio, Republican Fund-Raiser (see Child Pornography)

First Selectman Peter Dibble (Stonington, CT) (see Child Molestation)

Republican Party Chairman Donald Fleischman (Brown County, WI) (see Fondling)

Constable Larry Dale Floyd (R-TX) (see Enticement)

Councilman Jack W. Gardner (Millersville, PA) (see Child Molestation)

Richard Gardner Jr., Candidate for the Nevada Assembly (see Incest)

Mayor John Gosek (Oswego, NY) (see Soliciting Sex w/ a Minor)

Mayor Philip Giordano (Waterbury, CT) (see Assault, Sexual)

Mark A. Grethen, Conservative Activist (see Republican of the Year)

State Senator John Hathaway (R-ME) (see Statutory Rape)

Republican Party Chairman Paul Ingram (Thurston County, WA) (see **Incest**)

Earl "Butch" Kimmerling, Conservative Activist (see **Child Molestation**)

Judge Ronald C. Kline (see **Child Pornography**)

U.S. Representative Donald "Buz" Lukens (R-OH) (see **Delinquency of a Minor, Contributing to**)

Jon Matthews, Conservative Commentator (see **Indecent Exposure**)

State Delegate Robert McKee (R-MD) (see **Child Pornography**)

Nicholas Morency, Conservative Activist (see **Child Pornography**)

Republican Committee Chairman Jeffrey Patti (Sparta, NJ) (see **Child Pornography**)

DA Mark Pazuhanich (Monroe County, PA) (see **Fondling**)

Tom Randall, Republican Petitioner (see **Child Molestation**)

Republican Party Chairman Beverly Russell (Union County, SC) (see **Child Molestation**)

State Representative Larry Jack Schwarz (R-CO) (see **Pornography**)

Mark Seindensticker, Campaign Aide (see **Delinquency of a Minor, Contributing to**)

Tom Shortridge, Republican Political Consultant (see **Child Pornography**)

Councilman Fred C. Smeltzer, Jr. (Wrightsville, PA) (see **Rape of a Minor**)

Republican Party Chairman Robert "Bobby" Stumbo (Floyd County, KY) (see **Child Molestation**)

County Commissioner David Swartz (Richland, OH) (see **Battery, Sexual**)

Republican County Chair Armando Tebano (Schenectady County, NY) (see **Child Molestation**)

Robin Vanderwall, Conservative Activist (see **Soliciting Sex w/ a Minor**)

State Representative Keith Westmoreland (R-TN) (see **Indecent Exposure**)

Stephen White, Conservative Activist (see **Soliciting Sex w/ a Minor**)

PORNOGRAPHY

CONSERVATIVE COMMENTATOR AND FOX NEWS DARLING PREVIOUSLY STARRED IN GAY PORNOGRAPHY

Marine Reservist Mark Sanchez enrolled at Columbia University and was soon drawn into conservative activism. He filed formal discrimination complaints for students with military backgrounds, wrote an opinion piece for the *New York Post* about double standards of "diversity" and soon received invitations to appear on the conservative talk show circuit. Fox News booked him on *The O'Reilly Factor* and *Hannity and Colmes*, and he received encouragement from Newt Gingrich.[342]

On March 2, 2007, Sanchez accepted the Jeane Kirkpatrick Academic Freedom Award from the Conservative Political Action Conference, an event that made brief national news when Ann Coulter called Democratic presidential candidate John Edwards a "faggot."

After the award ceremony, it was revealed that Sanchez had previously acted in gay pornography under the pseudonyms

"Rod Majors" and "Pierre LaBranche"—appearing in more than 20 films.

Sanchez, star of "Touched by an Anal," "Butt Crack Mountain," and "Guys Who Swallow Cum," said in an interview that he was "pretty bad at being gay," and claimed to be working on a book titled "Gay Jihad: What the Radical Homosexual Movement Has In Store for You and Your Family."[343]

FORMER COLORADO STATE LEGISLATOR AND PAROLE BOARD OFFICIAL ACCUSED OF INCEST, GOES INTO PORNOGRAPHY BUSINESS

In 2001, Larry Jack Schwarz, who served in the Colorado State House from 1995 to 1997 and at the time was an appointed member of the Colorado Parole Board, was investigated after a female relative accused him of incest. The woman claimed he made her watch pornography starting at the age of four and had sex with her when she was 12. Schwarz could not be charged with incest because of the statute of limitations.

After Police searched Schwarz's house, they removed boxes of pornography, including child pornography. No charges were filed against Schwarz.[344]

After he was fired from his parole board position, Schwarz moved to California, where he and his wife work in his daughter's pornography company, Platinum X Pictures. Schwarz's daughter is the porn star Jewel De'Nyle, and the company manufactures and distributes her videos.[345]

Of his pornography job, Schwarz said:

"I feel no shame, as I have learned that what we do in our office is no different than any other business. It is the adult-entertainment industry, and it's not violent like what you see in real-life daily news or in mainstream movies."[346]

SEE ALSO:

Republican Party Chairman Beverly Russell (Union County, SC) **(Child Molestation)**

Supreme Court Justice Clarence Thomas **(Harassment, Sexual)**

PRIVATE

U.S. Representative Dan Burton (R-IN) (see **Adultery**)

Susan Carpenter-McMillan, Anti-Abortion Activist (see **Anti-Abortion**)

PROSTITUTION

CONGRESSMAN STOPPED BY POLICE APPARENTLY ENGAGED IN SEXUAL ACTIVITY WITH PROSTITUTE IN CAR, BLAMES IT ON STRESS FROM DIVORCE, LATER SUED BY WIFE FOR UNPAID ALIMONY

In November 1993, U.S. Congressman Ken Calvert (R-CA) was detained by police who found him "apparently engaged in sexual activity" with Lore Lindberg, a woman who had twice been arrested for prostitution. According to the police report, Calvert tried to drive away several times. The police claimed that they could not prove that Calvert had done anything illegal. No charges were filed.[347]

Calvert denied knowing that Lindberg was a prostitute. Lindberg backed up this story, claiming that she was not working that night.[348]

Initially, the police refused to release any details about the incident. The *Press-Enterprise* filed lawsuits to force the department to release the report. Before the report was released, Calvert maintained that "nothing happened."[349]

After a court ordered the police to release details about the incident, Calvert issued a statement blaming his actions on stress, maintaining his innocence, and claiming that the event was "personal":

> It is not part of my nature to talk publicly about my private life or my problems. I know that I have been very fortunate in my life, and that many people have problems which make mine seem minuscule in comparison. I have never felt that I had any reason to complain, or any excuses for failure. But, in retrospect, I realize now that this, or a similar incident, was probably inevitable.
>
> In the 15 months prior to the incident, my father had committed suicide, my wife of 15 years had asked for a divorce, and I had left the only home I had ever really known to go to Congress. And I convinced myself that everything was fine, and that I could handle all of these eruptions in my life. Obviously, I was very wrong.
>
> Looking back, it is clear that the timing of the incident was crucial. I had just returned home from my first session in Congress. It had been a grueling week—marathon sessions in Washington, followed by a Thanksgiving filled with memories of my father and thoughts of my marriage which had ended officially only a few weeks previous. I was feeling many emotions, but mostly, I was feeling intensely lonely.[350]

Calvert was given high marks by the Family Research Council, a leading Christian-Right think tank and lobbying firm, and once declared on the House floor that "we can't forgive what happened between the President and Ms. Lewinsky."[351]

Ex-Wife Filed for, Then Withdrew, Petition for Temporary Restraining Order, Claimed Calvert Harassed her, Failed to Pay Alimony

In October 1996, Calvert's ex-wife, Robin Lou Calvert, filed for a temporary restraining order against Calvert, claiming that he had harassed her. At the time, the pair was engaged in a public battle over whether Calvert had made all of his alimony payments. Calvert withdrew her petition for the restraining order later the same day.[352]

Two weeks earlier, Calvert filed a lawsuit against Robin Lou alleging she had lied when she got the court to garnish his congressional wages to pay $9,000 in alimony she claimed he owed. Calvert maintained that he did not owe her alimony.[353]

WASHINGTON STATE REPRESENTATIVE CAUGHT WITH GAY PROSTITUTE, REVEALED TO BE A CROSS-DRESSER

In October 2007, Washington Republican State Representative Richard Curtis was entangled in a gay prostitution scandal in Spokane. According to the police report, Curtis stopped at the Hollywood Erotic Boutique, a popular "meeting place" for men where Curtis was known as a regular, according to at least one employee. There, he met Cody Castagna, a part-time waiter and porn model, who asked him for a cigarette. Castagna asked Curtis, dressed in lingerie, if he "wanted to get together." Curtis did but warned that he wouldn't pay for sex, since that would constitute prostitution. Instead, he promised $100 to "help him out for gas."[354]

The two eventually returned to Curtis' room at the Davenport Hotel. Castagna used a condom on Curtis, who then offered Castagna $1,000 for "bareback sex." But Curtis only had $200 in cash, so the young man took his wallet hostage until he could come up with the rest.[355]

*[Washington State Representative] Curtis warned that he wouldn't pay
for sex, since that would constitute prostitution,
but offered $100 to help out for gas.*

A conservative husband and father who had made a political career out of voting against gay marriage, domestic partnerships, and anti-discrimination laws, Curtis immediately called the police and accused Castagna of extorting money from him. When police arrived, they found a nylon rope, a plastic stethoscope, and other items, which Curtis asked them to ignore.[356]

When the full story of how he had paid for gay sex inevitably hit the press, Curtis issued the statement, "I am not gay." Several days later, he resigned.[357]

ASSOCIATION OF EVANGELICALS PRESIDENT ADMITS TO "SEXUAL IMMORALITY" WITH MALE PROSTITUTE

In November 2006, homosexual prostitute Mike Jones alleged that he had taken methamphetamine and engaged in homosexual sex with Reverend Ted Haggard, the then-president of the National Association of Evangelicals and pastor of the New Life Church in Colorado Springs, Colorado. Jones claimed that the affair lasted three years.[358]

In the wake of the revelations, Haggard admitted to "sexual immorality," resigned his positions, and moved his family to Phoenix, Arizona, where he said he planned to pursue a degree in psychology.[359]

Following the scandal, Haggard entered "intensive counseling," in which one of the four ministers presiding dubbed him "completely heterosexual." He later revised his quote, pointing out that what he meant to say was that the therapy "gave Ted the tools to embrace his heterosexual side." By December of 2007, Haggard claimed that he was, in fact, "completely heterosexual" after all.[360]

Jones wrote a book detailing his relationship with Haggard, *I Had to Say Something: The Art of Ted Haggard's Fall.*[361]

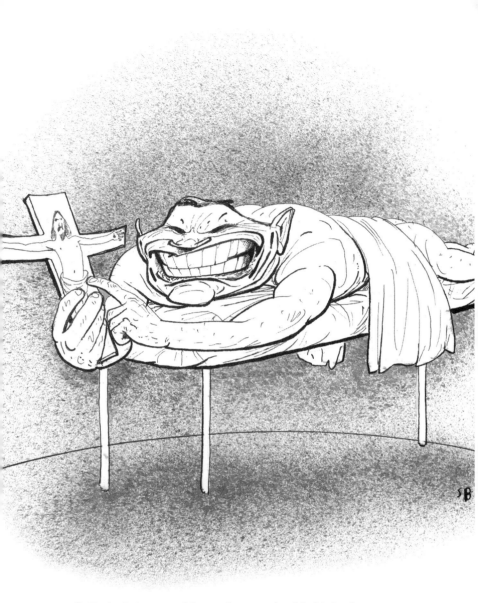

"We don't have to debate what we should think about homosexual activity. It's written in the Bible."
—*Ted Haggard*

Less Than One Year After His Resignation, Haggard E-mailed Supporters Asking for Money to Support Family, Claiming Family Would Move to Phoenix Halfway House

In August 2007, Haggard sent an e-mail to his supporters asking them to contribute tax deductible contributions to Families with a Mission to support his family's efforts at the Dream Center, a halfway house run by the Phoenix First Assembly of God. Haggard claimed that his family would move to the Dream Center and that he and his wife needed support as they worked toward college degrees in psychology.[362]

Tommy Barnett, the pastor of the church that operates the halfway house, claimed that Haggard had spoken prematurely and that he would not be working at the Dream Center. According to *The Gazette*, "Barnett is one of three pastors assigned to help with Haggard's spiritual restoration."[363]

Non-Profit Director Says He Did Not Authorize Haggard's E-mail; Director Previously Charged with Sexual Crimes, Now Registered Sex Offender

Paul G. Huberty, the executive director of Families with a Mission denied that the organization was soliciting contributions for Haggard. According to an e-mail from Huberty:

> *"Our non-profit organization never authorized a mass public appeal for donations for the Haggard family, nor were we even aware of it until published by the media. Not one donation has been solicited by our non-profit organization designated to or supporting the Haggard family—and our organization has not sent any solicited financial support to Pastor Haggard."*[364]

According to *The Gazette*, Huberty was convicted in 1996 of "consensual sodomy, fondling his genitals in public, indecent acts and adultery," dismissed from the military (he was an 18-year veteran), and sentenced to six months in confinement. The sodomy, indecency, and adultery charges involved a 17-year-old girl who was his legal ward at the time. Huberty was also convicted of "second-degree attempted sexual assault in January 2004," and his sentence included "stipulations that he not contact minors over the Internet, visit area schools, or possess pornography."[365]

U.S. SENATOR'S PHONE NUMBER FOUND IN RECORDS OF INDICTED D.C. MADAM

In July 2007, Republican U.S. Senator David Vitter apologized for "a very serious sin in my past" after his telephone number turned up in phone records of alleged D.C. Madam Deborah Jeane Palfrey. Vitter's number appeared in the records five times between 1999 and 2001. Palfrey was under federal criminal indictment for money laundering and racketeering related to an alleged D.C.-based prostitution ring.[366]

After the revelation about Vitter's ties to the prostitution ring, Jeannette Maier, who pleaded guilty in 2002 to running the Canal Street brothel in New Orleans, claimed Vitter was a "frequent customer" of the brothel in the 1990s.[367]

Vitter initially dropped out of sight for a week before appearing at a press conference where he refused to discuss details of the allegations but admitted to past sins for which God and his wife had forgiven him. Vitter claimed that he and his wife believed in "important values" and that he was trying to live up to those values:

> *"If continuing to believe in those values causes some to attack me because of my past failures, then so be it."*[368]

D.C. Madam Threatens to Have Vitter Subpoenaed in Criminal Case

Palfrey said in July 2007 that she would have her lawyers call Vitter as a witness if her case went to trial:

> *"It can only help my case.*

"I don't think he would ever get onto a witness stand and acknowledge committing a crime. That would be the final blow for him."[369]

Facing 55 years in prison, Palfrey committed suicide in April 2008.[370]

Two Months Later, New Orleans Prostitute Alleges Five-Month Relationship with Vitter

In 2007, Wendy Yow Ellis, a New Orleans prostitute, alleged that Vitter paid her for sex "several times a week" from July to November 1999. Ellis' allegations were revealed by Larry Flynt. Ellis claimed that she passed a lie detector test. Ellis worked through the New Orleans Escort Service.[371]

SEE ALSO:

Alfred Bloomingdale, Reagan Advisor **(S&M)**

U.S. Senator Larry Craig (R-ID) **(Men's Rooms)**

Richard A. Dasen, Sr., Conservative Activist **(Rape)**

Mayor Philip Giordano (Waterbury, CT) **(Assault, Sexual)**

State Representative Brent Parker (R-UT) **(Groping of Law Enforcement Officials)**

PRUDE

ATTORNEY GENERAL ORDERS
LADY JUSTICE STATUE'S BREAST COVERED

In 2002, Attorney General John Ashcroft felt uncomfortable being photographed in front of a statue in the Department of Justice. The art-deco piece, created by sculptor C. Paul Jennewein, was commissioned in 1933 for $7,275. It depicts Lady Justice in

*The art deco piece . . . depicts Lady Justice in a toga but . . .
the figure's right breast is exposed. [Attorney General] Ashcroft
ordered the statue draped.*

a toga but, contrary to Ashcroft's convictions regarding pornography, the figure's right breast is exposed.[372]

Ashcroft ordered the statue draped, and the Justice Department forked out $8,000 in taxpayer funds for blue curtains to protect Ashcroft's artistic sensibilities.[373]

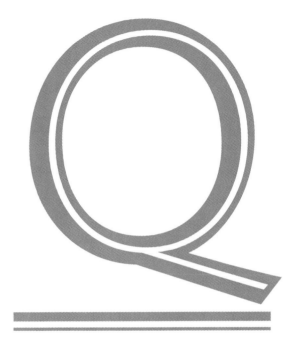

"All I'll say is that I've led a human life."[374]

—Representative NEWT GINGRICH (R-GA)

QUESTIONABLE EXPENSES

Mayor John Gosek (Oswego, NY) (see **Soliciting Sex w/ a Minor**)

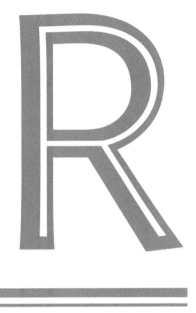

"When the wife does not focus in on the needs and the feelings—sexually, personally—to make him feel like a man, to make him feel like a success, to make him feel like her hero, he's very susceptible to the charm of some other woman. . . . The cheating was his decision to repair what's damaged and to feed himself where he's starving. But yes, I hold women accountable for tossing out perfectly good men by not treating them with the love and kindness and respect and attention they need."[375]

—DR. LAURA SCHLESSINGER,
Conservative Radio Host, on Eliot Spitzer's prostitution scandal

RAPE

PROMINENT BUSINESSMAN, CONSERVATIVE ACTIVIST, ADMITS TO SPENDING MORE THAN $1 MILLION ON PROSTITUTES AND USING NON-PROFIT DEBT AGENCY TO COERCE WOMEN AND GIRLS INTO SEX

In 2004, Richard A. Dasen, Sr., a prominent Kalispell, Montana, businessman, was arrested in a prostitution sting operation. He was found nearly naked in a cheap motel room with a 15-year-old girl and charged with her rape. Dasen was accused by many low-income, drug-addicted women of loaning them money through his non-profit, Christian Financial Counseling, and then forcing them to have sex with him when they were unable to pay him back. While investigators estimated a number five times greater, Dasen admitted to spending at least $1 million on prostitutes.[376]

Dasen was charged with 14 counts of prostitution and related charges.[377]

In 2007, the Montana State Supreme Court rejected Dasen's appeal of his 20-year sentence. Eighteen years of the sentence were suspended. Dasen got out of prison in May 2007.[378]

Local Christian Coalition Activist, and Republican Candidate for County Office Called Dasen "Incredibly Benevolent"

After his arrest, Denise Cofer, a local Christian Coalition activist and Republican candidate for county commissioner, called Dasen "incredibly benevolent" and noted that he was a "reliable supporter" of conservative causes:

> *"If there was a need in the community, he was there."*[379]

STATE LEGISLATOR AND SPONSOR OF TOUGHER SEX OFFENDER LAWS CHARGED WITH RAPING FOSTER DAUGHTERS

In July 2007, Ted Klaudt, a former South Dakota state legislator, was indicted on four counts of second-degree rape, two counts of sexual exploitation of a minor, one count of sexual contact with a child younger than 16, two counts of witness tampering, and one count of stalking.[380]

Court papers say Klaudt, a farmer and rancher, raped two foster daughters at his home and drove one of them to a remote location to take nude pictures.[381]

Klaudt coerced the girls into fake medical examinations under the pretext that he was checking them for possibly donating eggs to infertile couples. Both young women testified that Klaudt penetrated them with his fingers and a sex toy and touched their breasts.

Klaudt's lawyers argued that his actions did not amount to rape because the girls consented, while prosecutors countered that Klaudt's deception made any consent invalid.

The girls lived in Klaudt's home as part of a program that provides foster care for young people who have no safe home to return to after completing time in juvenile reform programs. One of the girls served as a legislative page, running errands for lawmakers.[382]

While serving in the state legislature, Klaudt helped sponsor several bills to increase the scope of and penalties for sex offenders, and co-sponsored a bill to prohibit distribution of contraceptives to high school students.[383]

Klaudt is serving a 54-year sentence at South Dakota State Penitentiary.[384]

During the Trial, Evidence Was Uncovered That Klaudt, Posing as a Modeling Agent, Attempted to Solicit Young Woman Online

State investigators who have analyzed Klaudt's computer say he attempted to solicit young girls online. He allegedly used the moniker "studman" in one occurrence to ask a 14-year-old girl to send him photos of herself, and the name "thephotoman" while posing as a 21-year-old modeling agent, requesting photos of a 15-year-old girl for a pornographic movie.

Authorities interviewed an 18-year-old who said Klaudt offered to take photographs of her and her 16-year-old sister with sex toys in order to build their modeling portfolios.[385]

PENNSYLVANIA BOROUGH COUNCILMAN ADMITTED TO RAPING TEENAGED DAUGHTER OF FRIEND

In September 2004, Fred Smeltzer, Jr., a Wrightsville Borough, Pennsylvania, councilman and deputy chief of the Wrightsville Fire Co., was charged with raping the 15-year-old daughter of a friend. Smeltzer gave the girl alcoholic beverages while on a campaign trip in Delaware and had sex with her.[386]

Smeltzer resigned his positions and pleaded no contest to the rape charge. He was sentenced to six months in jail and six months of house arrest.[387]

SEE ALSO:

Republican Party Chairman Paul Ingram (Thurston County, WA) *(Incest)*

REPUBLICAN OF THE YEAR

NOMINEE OF NRCC REPUBLICAN OF THE YEAR AWARD AT TIME SERVING 26 YEARS FOR SEX CRIMES AGAINST CHILDREN

In 2002, the National Republican Congressional Committee (NRCC) admitted that it had extended an invitation to Mark Grethen to receive a Republican of the Year Award, in Washington, D.C. The NRCC acknowledged its error in offering the award to Grethen, who at the time was serving 26 years in state prison for sex crimes against children, including "forcible sodomy, aggravated sexual battery and indecent liberties."[388]

Carl Foti, an NRCC spokesperson, said that the award had been rescinded and that the NRCC would donate $750 (the amount that Grethen had donated to the NRCC) to a victims' rights groups. According to Foti:

> *"We weren't aware of his current predicament. Otherwise, (the invitation) never would have been extended."*[389]

RUBBER SUITS

Rev. Gary M. Aldridge (see **Asphyxiation, Autoerotic**)

*"I want to share with you some information
about how God has called me to stand
in the gap, not only for others, but regarding
ethical and moral issues in our country."*[390]

—Dr. DAVID HAGER, FDA Advisor

S & M

ADVISOR TO RONALD REAGAN CARRIED ON LONG-TERM AFFAIR, PRACTICED S&M WITH MISTRESS AND PROSTITUTES

Alfred Bloomingdale helped bankroll Ronald Reagan's rise to power, then joined the new president's "kitchen cabinet" as one of a small group of close friends and advisors who helped shaped the California Republican's neoconservative policy. Heir to his family's department store fortune, Bloomingdale also used his money and connections to land prestigious positions on the Foreign Intelligence Advisory Board and the Advisory Commission on Public Diplomacy.[391]

Bloomingdale's young mistress, Vicki Morgan, encouraged some of his more bizarre sexual proclivities. At his second-ever lunch date with the 20-year-old movie usherette, the billionaire arrived with a hooker. On the drive from the restaurant, the hooker explained Bloomingdale's "special needs" in the bedroom and told her, "He won't hurt you much."[392]

When they arrived at the home of a dominatrix known as Mistress Kay, Morgan learned of Bloomingdale's fetishes, which involved watching lesbian S&M, then joining in himself with whips and belts. The two continued their affair for 12 years, while Bloomingdale set her up in a nice house, with a car, and a $10,000-per month allowance. The couple continued to visit Mistress Kay, along with a host of other dominatrices and prostitutes. For his 54th birthday, Morgan hired 15 hookers for her boyfriend. She claimed she acted as something of a therapist for Bloomingdale, helping him "overcome his Marquis de Sade complex."[393]

After being caught by his wife outside a Beverly Hills salon, Bloomingdale called off the affair. Morgan sued him, claiming that he had made oral obligations to support her financially. The case was thrown out of court. Then, shortly before his death from throat cancer, the billionaire heir stipulated that Morgan continue to receive payments after he died.[394]

SATANIC RITUAL ABUSE

Republican Party Chairman Paul Ingram (Thurston County, WA) (see **Incest**)

SEX ADDICTION

Judge Ronald C. Kline (see **Child Pornography**)

SEX CLUBS

REPUBLICAN NOMINEE FOR U.S. SENATE FORCED TO RESIGN AFTER SEALED DIVORCE RECORDS REVEALED EX-WIFE SAID HE WANTED HER TO HAVE SEX WITH HIM AT SEX CLUBS

In 2004, Jack Ryan, the Republican candidate for the U.S. Senate in Illinois, was forced to resign after a judge unsealed his divorce records, which contained allegations that he asked his ex-wife to have sex with him in public at sex clubs:[395]

> "Respondent wanted me to have sex with him there, with another couple watching. I refused. Respondent asked me to perform a sexual activity upon him, and he specifically asked other people to watch. I was very upset. We left the club and

respondent apologized, said that I was right and he would never insist that I go to a club again. He promised it was out of his system."

However, Ryan again took his wife to what he called an "avant-garde nightclub" in Paris, according to the court records. He claimed neither of them felt comfortable there and soon left.[396]

Ryan's campaign had previously come under scrutiny for having a campaign worker follow his opponent, Barack Obama, around the clock.[397]

SEX TOURS

DURING NASTY DIVORCE, PRESIDENT'S BROTHER ADMITS TO SEX WITH WOMEN WHO CAME TO HIS HOTEL ROOMS IN ASIA

In 2002, according to Sharon Bush, Neil Bush's ex-wife, Bush informed her via e-mail that he wanted a divorce. This touched off a nasty and publicly waged divorce battle that included allegations of extra-marital affairs, allegations that Bush had fathered a child with the woman he married after his divorce, and an admission by Bush that he slept with women in Thailand and Hong Kong who came to his door unsolicited. Bush maintained that he did not pay the women for sex.[398]

Many of the allegations were revealed in a March 2003 deposition that Bush gave for his divorce proceedings:

"Mr. Bush," attorney Marshall Davis Brown said to him, "you have to admit that it's a pretty remarkable thing for a man just to go to a hotel room door and open it and have a woman standing there and have sex with her." [399]

175

Bush admitted to sleeping with women in Thailand and
Hong Kong who came to his door "unsolicited."

"It was very unusual," Bush agreed, admitting that it had happened several times. "I don't remember the exact number."

Sharon also claimed that her husband had fathered a two-year-old daughter with his new girlfriend, an aide to his mother, former First Lady Barbara Bush. The judge denied a request for a DNA test. [400]

SEXUAL EXPLOITATION OF A MINOR

YOUTH MINISTER PRAISED BY BUSH ADMITS TO HAVING SEX WITH TEENAGED GIRL HE WAS COUNSELING

In October 2004, President George W. Bush signed a bill in Des Moines, Iowa, extending tax cuts, including the child tax credit and the elimination of the marriage penalty. Bush, who was campaigning for re-election, singled out Mike and Sharla Hintz (and their four children aged four to eight) as beneficiaries of the extension. According to Bush:

> "Under all the tax relief we've passed, they saved about $2,800 last year. With this extra money, they bought a wood-burning stove to reduce their home heating costs.
>
> "They also made home repairs and improvements. They took the family on a vacation to Minnesota. Next year when you get your check, you may want to come to Texas. Without the tax bill I'm signing . . . the Hintzes would have paid $1,200 more in federal taxes next year." [401]

At the time, Mike Hintz was the youth pastor at the First Assembly of God Church in Clive, Iowa. The *Des Moines Register* reported that he was a Republican. [402]

Two months later, Hintz was arrested for having sex with a 17-year-old girl in his youth group. At the time, he was counseling her for emotional and behavioral problems. He ultimately admitted to having sex with her on several occasions.[403]

In March 2005, Hintz pleaded guilty to three charges of sexual exploitation by a counselor. Hintz was sentenced to two years' probation, was required to pay restitution to his victim, to attend a sex offender treatment program, and to register as a sex offender.[404]

SKINNY-DIPPING

Jon Grunseth, Minnesota Gubernatorial Candidate
(see Adultery*)*

SODOMY, NONCONSENSUAL

WHITE HOUSE FDA APPOINTEE ACCUSED BY EX-WIFE OF ABUSE DURING MARRIAGE, FORCING HER TO HAVE ANAL SEX

In 2005, Dr. David Hager, a White House appointee to the FDA advisory committee for reproductive health drugs and the author of such books as *Stress and the Woman's Body* and *As Jesus Cared for Women*, was accused by his ex-wife, Linda Davis, of abuse during their marriage, including forcing her to have anal sex. Hager was interviewed in 2002 by the White House as a candidate for surgeon general.[405]

Davis' accusations were made in an article in *The Nation.* Davis said she came forward with her allegations because "there needed to be some public accountability for these actions."[406]

"I probably wouldn't have objected so much, or felt it was so abusive if he had just wanted normal [vaginal] sex all the time.... But it was the painful, invasive, totally nonconsensual nature of the [anal] sex that was so horrible," Hager's wife said.

Hager sometimes complained that he couldn't feel the difference.

"Well then," she advised her gynecologist husband, "you're in the wrong business."

Hager later began paying his wife for sex acts that she wouldn't normally engage in, such as anal and oral sex. In 1995, Hager's wife was diagnosed with narcolepsy. For the next seven years, Hager sodomized his wife without her blessing while she slept.

"My sense is that he saw [my narcolepsy] as an opportunity," she said.[407]

Hager denied the accusations:

"As I said before, the allegations as stated do not reveal all of the information and therefore they're incomplete and not true.

"No one likes to be criticized, no one likes to be torn apart privately or publicly and I think that it's disappointing that my former wife has chosen this avenue to vent her anger and bitterness."[408]

Hager, a member of Focus on the Family's Physician Resource Council and the Christian Medical and Dental Society, was an anti-abortion activist before his appointment, and he opposed the FDA proposal to make Plan B an over-the-counter drug.[409]

After being informed by *The Nation* of Davis' accusations, Janice Shaw Crouse of Concerned Women for America, the group Hager had helped petition for a ban of the abortion pill, stuck by her earlier support of him:

"He has been a gentleman," Crouse said. "He is a person of character and integrity, and I think people admire that."[410]

SEE ALSO:

Mark A. Grethen, G.O.P. Activist and Donor (Republican of the Year)

SODOMY, STATUTORY

REPUBLICAN COMMITTEEMAN ADMITS TO HAVING SEX WITH MAN, CLAIMS UNAWARE MAN WAS UNDERAGE

In December 2002, Andrew Buhr was arrested and charged with having sex with an underage male teenager. Buhr was elected as a Hadley Township, Missouri, committeeman in 2000 and had previously served as a member of the St. Louis City Republican Central Committee. Hadley ran as the Republican nominee for the Missouri House for District 84 in 2000.[411]

At the trial, the victim claimed that he had sex with Buhr after meeting in the steam room of a St. Louis County health club. The boy suggested they find another place and led Buhr to a restroom near the local high school. Afterward, when they returned to Buhr's car, the boy told Buhr that his mother would pick him up.[412]

Buhr's first trial ended in a hung jury. In his second trial he was acquitted after his attorney argued that he was unaware that the boy he had sex with was underage. Buhr's lawyer argued that Buhr assumed the boy was 18, because he had met him at the gym, in a room with a sign on the door that specified you had to be 18 or older to be there.[413]

Lost Presidential Appointment After Arrest

Buhr was appointed by President George W. Bush to the Commission on Presidential Scholars in November 2002 but lost his position within a month after his arrest.[414]

SOLICITING SEX W/A MINOR

FLORIDA FEDERAL PROSECUTOR COMMITS SUICIDE WHILE IN JAIL, ACCUSED OF SOLICITING SEX WITH FIVE-YEAR-OLD

In September 2007, John David "Roy" Atchison was arrested at the Detroit airport after soliciting sex with a minor from an undercover FBI agent. Atchison thought he had arranged to have sex with the woman's five-year-old daughter. When he was arrested he had a Dora the Explorer doll, hoop earrings, and petroleum jelly for the child. In their online conversation, Atchison assured the mother how tenderly he treated children:

> *"I'm always gentle and loving; not to worry; no damage ever; no rough stuff ever ever. . . . I've done it plenty."*[415]

Atchison was a federal prosecutor for the North District of Florida. He was married with three children, and served as president of a youth sports organization in his community.[416]

In October 2007, after petitioning the court to take him off suicide watch, Atchison hung himself in the Milan, Michigan, federal prison.[417]

CONGRESSMAN AND "VOCIFEROUS GAY RIGHTS OPPONENT" SOLICITS SEX FROM TEENAGED GAY NUDE DANCER

In 1980, Representative Robert "Bob" Bauman was arrested and charged with soliciting sex from a 16-year-old male nude dancer in a gay bar. Bauman was caught in an FBI sting operation. Bauman pled guilty to a misdemeanor offense and received a six-month suspended sentence.[418]

Prior to his arrest, Bauman was a "vociferous gay rights opponent" and the head of the American Conservative Union. Bauman lost re-election in 1982.[419]

Bauman has said that the man he solicited for sex "was a hard-core street guy" and emphasized that he was not an innocent child:

> *"I want you to understand I wasn't robbing the playground."*[420]

Published Book in Which Claimed "Numerous Closet Gays" in Congress, Reagan Administration and Other Washington D.C. Power Circles

In 1986, Bauman published *The Gentleman from Maryland: The Conscience of a Gay Conservative,* in which he describes his "identity crisis" and claims that there were closeted gays "in Congress, the Reagan Administration and White House, the judiciary, the military and Washington power circles."[421]

Sued by Questionable Texas Foundation for "Absconding" with $700,000 in Grant Monies

In the 1980s, Bauman agreed to head two conservative foundations funded by Texas millionaire Shearn Moody, Jr. Federal prosecutors investigated whether Moody used the foundations to divert assets from his family's foundation, the Moody Foundation, and Moody eventually went to prison for bankruptcy fraud. Bauman received immunity from prosecution in exchange for his testimony against Moody. The Moody Foundation later sued Bauman, claiming he stole $700,000 in grant monies. A Texas judge ordered Bauman to pay $1.25 million in damages to the Moody Foundation.[422]

In 1993, Bauman declared personal bankruptcy. He had not paid the $1.25 million judgment that was listed as a liability in his bankruptcy.[423]

Asked to Testify Before Congress to Promote Sex Education in Schools

In 1995, Bauman wrote to Representative Peter Hoekstra (R-MI) to ask if he could testify in favor of sex education in schools. Bauman claimed that a lack of education on homosexuality led to his political demise:

"I'm a good example of what happened when no information is provided about homosexuality, it ruined my career. Everything that happened to me could have been modified in my life if I had had some education."[424]

GOP DIRECTOR OF ST. LOUIS ELECTION BOARD CAUGHT IN INTERNET SEX STING SOLICITING UNDERAGE GIRL

In 2005, Kevin Coan, the former Republican director of the St. Louis Election Board, pleaded no contest to "soliciting a sexual act over the Internet" from a girl he thought was 14 years old. He told the officers posing as 14-year-old girls that he would arrive at a designated grocery store in a "nice silver car," would be wearing a suit, and would have cash on hand. When he arrived, authorities recognized him by the picture he posted on the Internet chat site.[425]

In the plea agreement, the charge was reduced to a misdemeanor. According to the prosecutor, Coan's charge was reduced because he sought treatment and because a doctor determined he was unlikely to reoffend:

> *"This was a different type of case, it was unique, because (Coan) recognized that he had a problem and got treatment for it long before he had been ordered to do so."*[426]

OSWEGO, NEW YORK, GOP MAYOR CONVICTED OF SOLICITING SEX WITH UNDERAGE GIRLS; ALLEGED TO HAVE PROMISED DRUGS IN RETURN FOR SEX

In September 2005, Republican Oswego, New York, Mayor John Gosek was caught in a sting operation and arrested after he attempted to solicit sex with two 15-year-olds. According to the FBI, Gosek solicited sex with minors on several occasions and promised drugs in return for sexual favors.[427]

Although a federal judge let Gosek out on bail, he said there was "understandable concern" about Gosek's "deviant sexual urges," and he ordered a monitoring bracelet for Gosek and confined him to his home.[428]

In November 2005, Gosek was indicted on two counts of attempting to solicit sex from a minor. The charges stemmed from his arrest in the sting operation and from phone calls tapped by federal authorities in which he attempted to solicit sex with a girl he believed was 14 years old.[429]

In July 2006, Gosek was sentenced to 37 months in federal prison. His sentence was reduced from the minimum five years because he provided information to FBI agents in a corruption investigation. Gosek is serving his time at the Federal Correctional Complex in Butner, North Carolina.[430]

In an interview following his guilty plea, Gosek claimed that he never thought the girls would actually be in the hotel room and that he never took drugs. He blamed his behavior on addiction:

> *"Why didn't I stop drinking? Why didn't I stop having these conversations? If you have an addiction, if you're a drug addict or an addicted gambler or you're an alcoholic—if everybody could say, 'I'm not going to smoke anymore,' there'd be no lung cancer. But you know, I have those addictions."*[431]

Admits to Affair with City Hall Staffer Which Had Previously Denied

In March 2005, Cindi L. Harris, a former city employee, was caught speeding in a city-owned vehicle assigned to Gosek. Harris claimed she was Gosek's girlfriend but Gosek denied that was true.[432]

In a July 2006 interview with the *Post-Standard*, Gosek admitted to the affair with Harris but refused to say how many extramarital affairs he had conducted.[433]

Audit Found $3,500 in "Questionable or Unnecessary Expenses" by Mayor, Including Dinner at Hooters

After Gosek's arrest, New York State Comptroller Alan G. Hevesi audited Gosek's expenses as mayor and found $3,500 in "questionable or unnecessary expenses." One expense was a $25 bill at an Albany-area Hooters.[434]

REPUBLICAN STRATEGIST WITH TIES TO RALPH REED AND JACK ABRAMOFF SENTENCED TO SEVEN YEARS FOR SOLICITING SEX WITH MINORS ON THE INTERNET

In 2004, Robin Vanderwall was sentenced to 60 years in prison, with 53 years suspended, for soliciting sex with minors over the

Internet. Vanderwall was caught in an undercover sting operation after he contacted a Virginia police officer who was posing as an underage boy in an Internet chat room and asked the officer to meet him at a local park. When the 34-year-old conservative activist arrived, the cops arrested him. [435]

Vanderwall was found guilty at a bench trial in April 2004. Vanderwall had run several Virginia campaigns for Republican candidates. [436]

Later, during the Jack Abramoff investigation, it was revealed that Vanderwall was the executive director of the Faith and Family Alliance, which Abramoff and Ralph Reed had used to transfer Indian gaming money to conservative groups. [437]

MINISTER WHO CONDEMNED HOMOSEXUALS SENTENCED TO TEN YEARS IN PRISON FOR SOLICITING SEX FROM MALE TEEN

In January 2004, a jury found Philadelphia-based preacher Craig Stephen White guilty of criminal solicitation to commit involuntary deviate sexual intercourse. White was accused by a 14-year-old boy of twice approaching him while driving a minivan, first asking if the boy knew where he might find any strip clubs or adult bookstores, then soliciting him for oral sex. He offered the boy $20 to allow White to perform fellatio on him. [438]

White was a street preacher known as "Brother Stephen" who had worked extensively with children in his ministry. White was sentenced to four to ten years in prison. [439]

After the guilty verdict, the judge warned that White should not be allowed around children:

> *"He's a preacher, and he has access to children. This jury has spoken. He has been convicted of attempting to lure a child into a vehicle."* [440]

White, whose ministry focused on college campuses, had said that "sinners hang out" on campuses and had "vocally condemned Jews, Muslims, atheists and homosexuals."[441]

SEE ALSO:

Constable Larry Dale Floyd (R-TX) (Enticement)

STATUTORY RAPE

PRIMARY CANDIDATE FOR U.S. SENATE ACCUSED OF HAVING SEX WITH 12-YEAR-OLD BABYSITTER

In June 1996, Maine State Senator W. John Hathaway, who was in a three-way race for the Republican nomination for U.S. Senate, faced charges that he had sex with his 12-year-old babysitter multiple times over an 18-month period while he was living in Huntsville, Alabama.[442]

Hathaway admitted that he was questioned in 1990 by the Madison County, Alabama, district attorney (who was a Republican) on allegations of statutory rape but denied ever having sexual relations with his babysitter. Hathaway claimed that the girl was "mentally disturbed."[443]

The district attorney involved with the case said that he wanted to pursue the charges but that the girl came from a prominent family who did not wish to prosecute the case.[444]

After losing the Senate primary, Hathaway remained active in Republican politics, four years later serving as a delegate to the Republican National Convention in 2000 and as a fundraiser for George W. Bush.[445]

STETHOSCOPE

State Representative Richard Curtis (R-WA) (see
Prostitution)

SWINGERS

POLITICAL CONSULTANT POSTED WEB SITE ADS SOLICITING SEXUAL PARTNERS FOR HIM AND HIS WIFE

In 1996, compromising photos of political consultant Roger Stone emerged on Web sites where visitors go to solicit group sex. Stone was working on Republican presidential candidate Bob Dole's campaign at the time and had publicly criticized what he liked to call President Clinton's "zipper problem."[446]

The ads on the Web site included photos of "Stone stripped to the waist and his wife, a busty former model, topless or posing provocatively in a black teddy and stockings." They said they were looking for "couples or muscle-bound military men for group sex." One ad also described Stone's wife as "outrageously attractive with a 40DD-24-36 figure, violet eyes and a voracious sexual appetite." The couple was willing to "travel coast to coast and can meet in D.C., Miami, N.Y. City, L.A. or San Diego," according to the ad.[447]

Stone claimed that the photos, which had been appearing for several years, were the work of a "sick and disgruntled individual." Stone himself, however, had rented the post office box listed in the ads and paid the Web site to run the ads with his own credit card. He quit his job on Dole's campaign.[448]

In their Internet ad, political consultant Roger Stone and his wife said they were looking for "couples or muscle-bound military men for group sex."

"Frankly, history is an ongoing rebuke to secular left-wing values. They can't afford to teach history because it would destroy the core vision of a hedonistic America in which there is no past and there is no future."[449]

—Representative NEWT GINGRICH (R-GA)

TELEPHONE DATING SERVICE

CONGRESSMAN ABRUPTLY DROPS OUT OF RE-ELECTION RACE AFTER ALLEGATIONS SURFACED THAT HE HAD SOUGHT EXTRAMARITAL GAY SEX

In August 2004, U.S. Congressman Ed Schrock (R-VA) "abruptly" announced his retirement after a gay activist posted information on his Web site claiming Schrock "solicited sex from men on a telephone-dating service" and a telephone recording he claimed was Schrock's:[450]

> *"Uh, hi, I weigh 200 pounds, I'm 6'4"... blond hair...*
> *very muscular, very buffed up, uh very tanned, uh, I just like*
> *to get together with a guy from time to time just to, just to*
> *play,"* a transcript of the recording read. *"I'd like him to be*
> *in very good shape, flat stomach, good chest, good arms, well*
> *hung... just get naked, play, see what happens, nothing real*
> *heavy duty... go down on him, he can go down on me, and*
> *just take it from there... hope to hear from you. Bye."*[451]

Schrock, a retired navy officer and a Vietnam veteran, claimed that the allegations would prevent him from running a substantive campaign. Schrock said the unspecified allegations had "called into question my ability to represent the citizens of Virginia's Second Congressional District."[452]

Schrock had taken a consistent stance against gay rights in his career, voting to constitutionally ban gay marriage and for provisions to repeal the Clinton administration's "don't ask, don't tell" policy. "You're in the showers with them, you're in the bunk room with them, you're in the staterooms with them," Schrock complained to the *Virginian-Pilot*.[453]

Got Job as Congressional Committee Aide after Retirement

In December 2004, the *Richmond Times-Dispatch* reported that Schrock would work as a subcommittee staff director of the House Government Reform Committee, chaired by fellow Virginia Republican Congressman Tom Davis.[454]

"Acknowledging that you are basically the perpetrator of your mess of a life is admittedly very upsetting."[455]

—DR. LAURA SCHLESSINGER,
Conservative Radio Host

UNLAWFUL SEXUAL ACTIVITY

CONSERVATIVE COMMENTATOR ARRESTED FOR UNLAWFUL SEXUAL ACTIVITY WITH UNDERAGE GIRLS

Fueling the controversy raging around President Clinton's impeachment proceedings, political commentator "Republican Marty" Glickman wrote the following in his newsletter, *The Ugly Truth*:

> "... [A] rednecked, classless pervert named Clinton from a low rent state like Arkansas was tearing down all standards for the highest office in the land. ... Decency, morals, telling the truth, and standing accountable were all American values that were on the line. With a rapist, a liar, and a sexual harasser and his First Enabler Hillary Clinton in charge; the country and its children were perilously close to sinking beneath recovery." [456]

In 2001, Glickman was arrested for unlawful sexual activity with underage girls and charged with delivering them LSD. While out on bail and awaiting trial, he committed suicide.[457]

UNWANTED SEX ACTS

INDIANA GOP COUNTY CHAIR FACES CHARGES FOR PERFORMING UNWANTED SEX ACT ON ANOTHER MAN

In August 2007, Glenn Murphy, Jr., announced that he would resign as Clark County, Indiana, GOP chair and as president of theYoung Republican National Federation after he was accused of committing an "unwanted sex act on another man."[458]

The accuser claimed that he awoke to find Murphy performing oral sex on him. Murphy's attorney, Larry Wilder, claimed the act was consensual.[459]

Two days after the incident, Murphy and the accuser met to discuss what took place. The victim tape-recorded the conversation:

"I thought that you were awake. It's my fault," Murphy said. "I'm not laying this off on you. I'm trying to explain what happened."

"I don't know, dude," the victim replied. "Yeah, I don't know how you can possibly think that it was okay to do that, honestly."

"Dude, I wasn't in my right mind," Murphy replied. "I wasn't thinking."

According to an affidavit, Murphy asked that the man not file a formal complaint and even offered to help pay for his schooling.[460]

In April 2008, the prosecution attempted to enter, as evidence, three statements by alleged victims who claimed Murphy had performed similar actions upon them. A 26-year-old man stated he awoke to find Murphy fondling his genitals without consent in October 2006. In 1998, a 21-year-old man awoke to Murphy performing oral sex on him without consent while the three slept at his girlfriend's house. The man filed a complaint with the Clarksville Police Department, but criminal charges were never filed. In 1996, a 20-year-old man claimed that Murphy invited him to sleep in his room at his fraternity house, where he awoke to Murphy trying to masturbate him, again without consent.[461]

"No one, regardless of what party they serve, no one, regardless of what branch of government they serve, should be allowed to get away with these alleged sexual improprieties, and yet it is obvious to me . . . that a double standard does exist." [462]

—Representative DAN BURTON (R-IN)

VICTIMS

Children, Mules, Prostitutes, Undercover Officers, Park Rangers, Taxpayers, Wives, Watermelons, Mistresses, The American People, etc. . . .

"On the question of social intermingling of the races, our people draw the line." [463]

—Senator STROM THURMOND (R-SC)

WATERMELONS

Neal Horsley, Anti-Gay/Anti-Abortion Crusader (see
Bestiality)

WEDLOCK, CHILD OUT OF

NEW YORK CONGRESSMAN, ARRESTED FOR DRUNK DRIVING, ADMITS FATHERING CHILD WITH MISTRESS, AN AIR FORCE COLONEL; DID NOT PRACTICE WHAT HE PREACHED

In May 2008, Republican U.S. Representative Vito Fossella was revealed to be the proud father of a three-year-old girl named Natalie. Baby Natalie was the congressman's fourth child; his three previous children were with his wife, Mary Pat.

The secret life of the conservative legislator, a vociferous family-values proponent, began unraveling when he was arrested for drunk driving in Alexandria, Virginia, after running a red light. He was driving to his mistress's house from a White House celebration for the New York Giants. Slurring his words, his mouth stained with red wine, he told the arresting officers he was on his way to retrieve his sick daughter and take her to the hospital ("Not," in the words of *New York Times* columnist Gail Collins," a very good plan, from the daughter's point of view"). After being booked, Fossella summoned Natalie's mother to bail him out of jail.[464]

"Don Vito," as he was affectionately known around his home borough of Staten Island by his constituents—or "Cheato Vito," as the *New York Post* subsequently dubbed him—met air force Lieutenant Laura Shoaf on a congressional delegation trip to Malta in December 2002. Their friendship blossomed into a full-scale romance during a subsequent congressional junket to Spain the following year.

Republican Speaker of the House Dennis Hastert headed both congressional delegations. After some very public displays of affection between Fossella and Shoaf on the Iberian peninsula, Shoaf was transferred from her position as air force congressional liason to an intelligence desk job at the Pentagon. She left her husband, Guy Shoaf, in late 2003. She resigned her commission and changed her name to Laura Fay after becoming pregnant by Don Vito.[465]

"Giving new meaning to the term 'family values,'" the *New York Post* reported, "Vito's father, Vito Sr., as well as uncle Frank, are said to be paying child support for the youngest Fossella spawn, Natalie. The child's mother, Laura Fay, was driving a car registered to Fossella's dad, her baby's grandpa."[466]

In Congress, Fossella had voted in favor of a constitutional amendment to ban gay marriage, total elimination of federal funding for Planned Parenthood, and the impeachment of President Clinton. He had also crusaded for posting the Ten Commandments in public places (presumably including the one that prohibits adultery).[467]

A flabbergasted Fossella constituent, Stephanie Perritone, a 32-year-old stylist at Hair Express in the Grasmere section of Staten Island, told *New York Post* columnist Andrea Peyser: "It's not okay! They should practice what they preach."[468]

SEGREGATIONIST SOUTH CAROLINA SENATOR FATHERED AFRICAN AMERICAN GIRL'S CHILD

At age 22, Strom Thurmond fathered a child with a 16-year-old African American girl. He later became known for his harsh stance on race relations, including his record-breaking filibuster against a Civil Rights Act in 1957—he spoke against the bill for over 24 consecutive hours.[469]

Essie Mae Washington-Williams, 78, came forward in 2003 to announce her parentage. Thurmond never officially acknowledged the girl as family, but his family did after the Republican passed away later that same year.[470]

The senator and his daughter had seen each other on a regular basis, according to a 2006 memoir written by Washington-Williams, *Dear Senator: A Memoir by the Daughter of Strom Thurmond*.

SEE ALSO:

U.S. Representative Dan Burton (R-IN) **(Adultery)**

WHIPPED CREAM

U.S. Representative Bob Barr (R-GA) (see **Impeachment**)

WITNESS TAMPERING

Councilman John J. Collins (Eatontown, PA) (see **Assault, Sexual**)

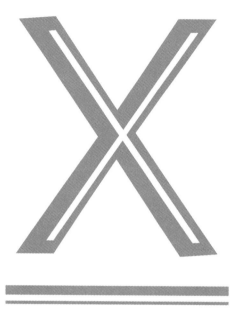

". . . a rednecked, classless pervert named Clinton from a low rent state like Arkansas was tearing down all the standards for the highest office in the land . . ." [471]

—Conservative Commentator "REPUBLICAN MARTY" GLICKMAN

X-RATED

(see **nude photos**)

XENOPHILIA

Neil Bush, First Son/Brother (see **Sex Tour**)

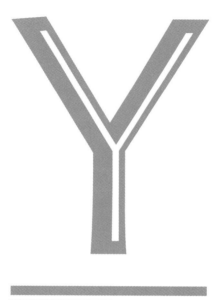

"Hit it from every angle. Open multiple fronts on your enemy, He must be confused, and feel besieged on every side . . ."[472]

—ROGER STONE, Republican Consultant

YOUTHFUL
INDISCRETION

U.S. Representative Henry Hyde (R–IL) (see **Impeachment, Advocates of Clinton's**)

"*I really believe that the pagans and the abortionists and the feminists and the gays and the lesbians who are actively trying to make that an alternative lifestyle, the ACLU, People for the American Way, all of them who try to secularize America. I point [the attacks of September 11] in their face and say, 'You helped this happen.'*" [473]

—JERRY FALWELL, to Pat Roberson on *The 700 Club*

ZOOLOGY

(see **Bestiality**)

NOTES

A

1 *New York Times*, "House Passes Bar to U.S. Sanction of Gay Marriage," July 13, 1996.

2 *Florida Times-Union*, "Governor-Hopeful Bowers Admits Decade-Long Affair," June 6, 1997.

3 Ibid.

4 *Southern Voice*, "Firing Gay Workers Still Legal in GA," January 26, 2007.

5 *Atlanta Journal and Constitution*, "Bowers Says He's Stopped Payments to Ex-Mistress," April 17, 1998.

6 Ibid.

7 Ibid.

8 Associated Press Online, "Rep. Dan Burton Admits to Affair," September 5, 1998.

9 Ibid.

10 *Salon*, "The Secret Lives of Republicans, Part One," September 11, 1998.

11 Ibid.

12 Dan Burton for Congress, "Awards," http://www.indiana-dan.com/our_congressman/dan_burton_awards.htm (accessed March 26, 2008).

13 *Salon*, "Lives of the Republicans, Part Two," September 16, 1998.

14 Ibid.

15 Ibid.

16 *Slate*, "Mr. Home-Wrecker Goes to Washington," May 8, 2007.

17 *Newsday,* "Rudy's $6.8 Million Goodbye," July 11, 2002.

18   Ibid.

19   Ibid.

20   *Slate*, "Mr. Home-Wrecker Goes to Washington," May 8, 2007.

21   *New York Daily News*, "The True Rudy," November 11, 2001; *Los Angeles Times*, "Ring Around the Rumors," March 5, 1997.

22   Associated Press, "Republican Drops Out of Governor's Race after Woman's Affair Claim," October 28, 1990.

23   Associated Press, "State Senator Who Admitted Affair Rejects Call for Resignation," September 16, 1998.

24   Ibid.

25   *New York Post*, "Giuliani's Bernard Kerik Shield," October 22, 2007.

26   *New York Times*, "Grand Jury Indicts Kerik on Corruption Charges," November 9, 2007.

27   *CBSNEWS.com*, "Skeletons Pour from Kerik's Closet," December 15, 2004.

28   *Vanity Fair*, "A Vast Right-Wing Hypocrisy," February 2008; *New York Times*, "Almost $2 Million Spent in Magazine's Anti-Clinton Project, but on What?" April 15, 1998.

29   *Vanity Fair*, "A Vast Right-Wing Hypocrisy," February 2008.

30   *Advocate*, "Awash in Whitewater," September 2, 1997; *Vanity Fair*, "A Vast Right-Wing Hypocrisy," February 2008.

31   *Fresno Bee*, "Thomas Affair Rolls off S. Valley," July 7, 2000.

32   *Washington Times*, "Inside Politics," June 27, 2000.

33   Ibid.

34   Ibid.

35   *Newsday*, "Drug Bill Author, Lobbyist Linked," June 27, 2000.

36   Citizens for Responsibility and Ethics in Washington, "World Bank President, Paul Wolfowitz, Responds to Criticism about His Romantic Interest's High Paying Job," April 9, 2007; *New York Post*, "Wolfowitz and Gal Pal Split Up," May 23, 2007.

37 Ibid.

38 Ibid.

39 Ibid.

40 *Slate*, "Susan Carpenter McMillan: The Woman Who Ate Paula Jones" September 21, 1997; *New York Times*, "Journal: Back to the Future," January 21, 1998.

41 *Slate*, "Susan Carpenter McMillan: The Woman Who Ate Paula Jones" September 21, 1997.

42 *New York Times*, "Journal: Back to the Future," January 21, 1998.

43 *ABC3340.com*, "Minister Found Dead in Montgomery Home," June 25, 2007.

44 *WSFA.com*, "Death Of Montgomery Minister Deeply Affects Snowdoun Pastor," August 28, 2007.

45 *Report of Autopsy*, "Evidence of Injury," Gary Michael Aldridge, Alabama Department of Forensic Sciences, Dictated June 26, 2007, www.thesmokinggun.com.

46 *Denver Post*, "Ex-Activist Faces New Child Sex Assault Counts," October 6, 2006.

47 Ibid.; Associated Press, "Appeals Court Rejects Former GOP Activist's Appeal in Sex Assault," April 28, 2005.

48 *Asbury Park Press*, "Sex-Case Teacher Arrested 3rd Time," August 3, 2005.

49 *Asbury Park Press*, "10-Year Term for Sex with Students," April 22, 2005.

50 *Asbury Park Press*, "Sex-Case Teacher Arrested 3rd Time," August 3, 2005.

51 *Asbury Park Press*, "Regional Week in Review," April 23, 2006.

52 *Asbury Park Press*, "Sex-Case Teacher Arrested 3rd Time," August 3, 2005.

53 *Pocono Record*, "Curtin's Wait Continues on New Trial Plea," April 19, 2007.

54 *Pocono Record*, "Prosecution Rests in Sex Trial against Committeeman," March 10, 2007.

55 Ibid.

56 *Pocono Record*, "Judge Grants Curtin Leniency in Sex Assault Case," June 19, 2007.

57 Associated Press, "Judge Rejects Ex-Conn Mayor's Bid for Reduced Sentence," August 6, 2007; Associated Press, "Giordano Pleads No Contest to State Child-Sex Charges," June 6, 2007.

58 Associated Press, "Judge Rejects Ex-Conn Mayor's Bid for Reduced Sentence," August 6, 2007.

59 *Hartford Courant*, "From Prison, A Bid for Pay," August 4, 2007.

60 *Connecticut Post*, "Giordano Jailed for 37 Years," June 14, 2003.

B

61 *Washington Post*, "A Chill in the Marble Halls: Others Fair Game for Scandal in Wake Of Clinton Affair," September 11, 1998.

62 Associated Press, "Publisher Cancels Reissue of Racy Novel by Lynne Cheney," April 3, 2004.

62a *Sisters*, by Lynne Cheney. Signet, 1981. Cited on *CNN.com*, The Situation Room Transcripts, October 30, 2006. http://transcripts.cnn.com/TRANSCRIPTS/0610/30/sitroom.03.html (accessed May 23, 2008).

63 Associated Press, "Texas Candidate Wrote Racy Romance Novel," October 24, 2006.

64 *The Apprentice*, by Lewis Libby. Thomas Dunne Books, 2001. Pg. 81.

65 *The Apprentice*, by Lewis Libby. Thomas Dunne Books, 2001. Pg. 79.

66 *Entertainment Weekly*, "Those Who Trespass," February 20, 2004; *Those Who Trespass*, by Bill O'Reilly. Onyx, 1999. Pg. 156.

67 *Those Who Trespass*, by Bill O'Reilly. Onyx, 1999. Pg. 156.

68 Ibid. Pg. 156–7.

69   Ibid. Pg. 157.

70   Ibid. Pg. 158.

71   Ibid. Pg. 306.

72   *News4Jax.com,* "Former Trinity Pastor Back in Jail on New Sex Charge," July 6, 2006; *First Coast News,* "Former Pastor Dr. Robert Gray in Court Again," August 15, 2006.

73   *First Coast News,* "Trinity Reacts to Dr. Bob Gray's Passing," November 11, 2007.

74   *Charlotte Observer,* "Dad's Beliefs Shaped During Time in Jail," March 27, 2005.

75   *Chicago Tribune,* "Man Charged with Threatening Doctor," June 2, 1999.

76   *Mansfield News Journal,* "More Charges for Swartz?" March 4, 2004.

77   *Mansfield News Journal,* "Swartz Enters Guilty Plea," February 3, 2004.

78   Associated Press, "Ex-County Commissioner Gets Eight Years in Abuse Case," April 2, 2004.

79   *Seattle Weekly,* "Closing the Barn Door," November 9, 2005.

80   *Salon,* "Hideous Kinkies," May 13, 2005.

81   *Esquire,* "Neal Horsley and the Future of the Armed Abortion Conflict," February 1, 1999.

82   Ibid.

83   Ibid.

C

84   *Vanity Fair,* "Red State Babylon," November 2006.

85   *Seattle Post-Intelligencer,* "Gay Sex Scandal Rocks Spokane," May 6, 2005.

86   Ibid.

87   Ibid.

88   Ibid.

89   *New York Times,* "Scars of a Sting Operation Prove to be Permanent," November 14, 2006.

90   *Seattle Post-Intelligencer,* "Gay Sex Scandal Rocks Spokane," May 6, 2005.

91 Ibid.
92 *Portland Press-Herald*, "Town Clerk Denies Assault," November 13, 1998.
93 *Boothbay Register*, "M. Robert Barter Indicted by Grand Jury," November 12, 1998.
94 *Oregonian*, "Christian Leader Did Touch Girls," August 16, 2006.
95 Ibid.
96 Associated Press, "Christian Coalition Leader Won't Face Molestation Charges," November 16, 2005.
97 *Oregonian*, "Christian Leader Did Touch Girls," August 16, 2006.
98 *Daily News of Los Angeles*, "Assembly Aide Denies Molesting 12-Year-Old," November 27, 2001.
99 Ibid.
100 *Daily News of Los Angeles*, "Civic Leader Faces Jail," August 20, 2002.
101 *Pensacola News Journal*, "Sex Offender John Burt Gets 18-Year Prison Sentence," May 13, 2004; *Pensacola News Journal*, "Burt Found Guilty of Molesting Girl," April 2, 2004; Associated Press, "Milton Abortion Protester Jailed after Losing Molestation Appeal," July 28, 2005.
102 *Pensacola News Journal*, "Wanted: Missing Abortion Foe," June 10, 2003.
103 Ibid.
104 *Honolulu Advertiser*, "Ex-Councilman Gets Year in Jail," August 18, 2000; *Honolulu Advertiser*, "Kona Man Faces Jail Term for Sexual Assault of Boy," July 21, 2000.
105 Associated Press, "Political Consultant Convicted of Child Sex Assault," June 28, 2006.
106 *McAllen Monitor*, "Defendant Expected to Take Stand in Sexual Harassment Case," June 21, 2006.
107 Ibid.
108 Associated Press, "Former Stonington First Selectman Gets Probation in Plea Bargain," June 3, 2004; Associated Press, "Town Official Charged with Risk of Injury," March 30, 2004.

109 Associated Press, "Former Stonington First Selectman Gets Probation in Plea Bargain," June 3, 2004.

110 Ibid.

111 *Intelligencer Journal* [Lancaster, PA], "Four Vie for Millersville Mayoralty," June 25, 2003.

112 Ibid.

113 Associated Press, "Opponents of Mary's Adoption by a Gay Man Won, the Child Lost," April 2, 2000.

114 *Indianapolis Star*, "Man Gets 40-Year Term for Molesting Adopted Girl," February 10, 2000.

115 Associated Press, "Opponents of Mary's Adoption by a Gay Man Won, the Child Lost," April 2, 2000.

116 *Orange County Register*, "Register Watchdog Report," May 27, 2006.

117 Ibid.

118 *New York Times*, "Journal: Beverly Russell's Prayers," August 2, 1995.

119 *Atlanta Journal and Constitution*, "Smith Case Put To Rest with Southern Graciousness," August 6, 1995.

120 *Orlando Sentinel*, "Charity Overwhelms Reason In Union, S.C.," November 1, 1995.

121 Ibid.

122 *Greenville News*, "Susan Smith's Stepfather to Continue Supervised Visits with His Son," June 16, 1999.

123 *Lexington Herald Leader*, "Around Kentucky: Ex-GOP Official Faces Sex Charge," October 4, 2005.

124 *Times Union* [Albany, NY], "GOP Official Faces Sex Charge," June 10, 2006; *Times Union*, "Former Politician Faces Trial," February 7, 2007.

125 *Times Union*, "Ex-County Aide Cuts Deal in Groping Case," February 8, 2007.

126 Ibid.

127 Ibid.

128 Ibid.

129 *Chicago Tribune*, "Green Oaks' Mayor Faces Child Pornography Charge," July 25, 2006; *Chicago Tribune*, "Ex-Green Oaks Mayor Denies Kid Porn Charges," August 30, 2006.

130 *Chicago Tribune*, "Official Called Judge in Porn Case," July 26, 2007.

131 *Chicago Tribune*, "Lawyer Seeks Dismissal of Child-Porn Case against Former Lake County Official," September 18, 2007.

132 *Virginian-Pilot* [Norfolk, VA], "Beach Man Sentenced in Child Porn Case," November 17, 2001.

133 Ibid.

134 Associated Press, "Virginia's Republican Electors Will Stick with Their Votes for Bush," November 8, 2000.

135 *San Jose Mercury News*, "Clinton Antagonist Nailed for Lewd Photos of Girl," April 25, 2003; *Washington Post*, "GOP Activist Admits to Child Porn," April 24, 2003.

136 *San Jose Mercury News*, "Clinton Antagonist Nailed for Lewd Photos of Girl," April 25, 2003.

137 *Washington Post*, "GOP Activist Admits to Child Porn," April 24, 2003.

138 *Los Angeles Times*, "Ex-Judge Collapses at Sentencing," February 21, 2007.

139 Ibid.

140 Ibid.

141 *Metropolitan News-Enterprise*, "Ex-Judge Ronald C. Kline Faces Prison Term after Guilty Plea to Child Pornography Charges," December 14, 2005.

142 *Los Angeles Times,* "Ex-Judge Collapses at Sentencing," February 21, 2007.

143 Ibid.

144 *Baltimore Sun*, "Official Resigns in Wake of Probe," February 16, 2008.

145 *Herald-Mail*, "Text of Del. Robert A. McKee's Letter of Resignation," February 16, 2008.

146 *Philadelphia Inquirer*, "Man Gets Federal Term for Child Porn," June 23, 2001.

147 *Star-Ledger* [Newark, NJ], "Porn Case Defendant: I'm Still GOP Chair," February 11, 2005.

148 *Star-Ledger*, "Child-Porn Ruling Lets Attorney Avoid Trial," April 13, 2006.

149 Ibid.

150 City News Service, "Political Consultant Pleads No Contest to Criminal Charges," June 13, 2001.

151 Ibid.

152 *Daily Breeze* [Torrance, CA], "Shortridge Enters Plea of Not Guilty," April 6, 2001.

153 *Times Leader* [Wilkes-Barre, PA], "Sherwood 'Sorry' for Pain to Family," May 4, 2005.

154 Ibid.

155 Associated Press, "Maryland Woman Files $5.5 Million Suit Against Rep. Sherwood," June 17, 2005.

156 Ibid.

157 *Centre Daily Times* [State College, PA], "President Stumps for Congressman Tainted by Affair," October 20, 2006.

158 Ibid.

159 Ibid.

160 Ibid.

161 *Boston Herald*, "Judge Quits after DUI Bust," February 16, 2008.

162 *Seattle Times*, "Candidate's Crossdressing Adds to GOP Race in Texas," April 13, 2004.

D

163 *Philadelphia Inquirer*, "Man Gets Federal Term for Child Porn," June 23, 2001.

164 Associated Press, "Former Congressman Begins Jail Term on Sex Conviction," January 2, 1991.

165 *Columbus Dispatch*, "Woman Sues Lukens Again for Damages," November 11, 1994.

166 Associated Press, "Former Congressman Begins Jail Term on Sex Conviction," January 2, 1991; *Columbus Dispatch*, "Woman Sues Lukens Again for Damages," November 11, 1994.

167 *Columbus Dispatch*, "Lukens Gets 30 Months in Prison for Corruption," June 20, 1996.

168 Ibid.

169 *Concord Monitor*, "Sex Offender Gets Year for Teen 'Party' Proposal," March 11, 2006; *Union Leader* [Manchester, NH], "Burton Aide Has Long Record," September 23, 2005.

170 New Hampshire Superior Court, Case 92-5-526.

171 *Union Leader*, "Burton Aide Has Long Record," September 23, 2005.

172 Ibid.

173 Ibid.

E

174 *New Orleans Times-Picayune*, July 10, 2007.

175 *Dallas Morning News*, "Constable Faces Sex Charges," July 30, 2005.

176 Ibid.

177 *Dallas Morning News*, "Denton Official Faced Child Sex Inquiry in '02," August 5, 2005.

178 *Dallas Morning News*, "DA's Lawsuit Seeks to Remove Constable Denton County," August 26, 2005.

179 *Pueblo Chieftain*, "DA Says Suspect's Sex History Relevant to Case," April 7, 2006.

180 *Fort Worth Star-Telegram*, "Former Official is Given 6 to Life," January 25, 2007.

181 *Dallas Morning News*, "Brief: Ex-Denton Constable Pleads Guilty to Child Porn Charges," September 1, 2007.

182 *Washington Post*, "Ethics Pressure Squeezes a Few Out the Door," May 2, 2005.

183 *Boston Globe*, "White House Reporter Under Scrutiny," February 2, 2005.

184 *Washington Post*, "Online Reporter Quits after Liberals' Expose," February 10, 2005.

185 *Washington Post*, "Jeff Gannon Admits Past 'Mistakes,' Berates Critics," February 19, 2005.

186 Ibid.

187 *New York Daily News*, cited in *The Brotherhood of the Disappearing Pants*, by Joseph Minton Amann and Tom Breuer. Nation Books, 2007. Pg. 103.

188 *OC Weekly*, "The Secret Lives of Bob Dornan," October 17, 1996.

F

189 Associated Press, "Rep. Hyde Admits Affair in 60s," September 17, 1998.

190 *Salon*, http://archive.salon.com/politics/feature/2000/09/04/cuss_word/ (acccessed May 21, 2008).

191 *Green Bay Press Gazette*, "Brown County Republican Party Chairman Faces Sex Charges," October 13, 2007.

192 Ibid.

193 Ibid.

194 *Green Bay Press Gazette*, "Ex-GOP Chair in Court on Sex Charges," March 7, 2008.

195 *Times Leader*, "Cops: Pazuhanich Fondled Girl," December 6, 2003.

196 *Times Leader*, "Judge Takes Parental Rights from Pazuhanich," December 26, 2003; *Pocono Record*, "PA Supreme Court Disbars Ex-Judge, DA," November 21, 2006.

197 *Morning Call* [Allentown, PA], "Girl, 10, Tells of Fondling by Judge," January 23, 2004.

198 *Morning Call*, "Judge Pleads and Gives Up Bench," July 13, 2004; *Morning Call*, "Pazuhanich Denies Groping Girl," January 8, 2004.

199 *Morning Call*, "Ex-Judge Barred for Life from Bench," October 6, 2004; *Times Leader*, "State Court Disbars Ex-Judge," November 21, 2006.

200 *Morning Call*, "Pazuhanich to Face Court from New Perspective," July 11, 2004.

201 *Arkansas Times,* "Dumond Case Revisited," September 1, 2005.

202 Ibid.

203 Ibid.

204 *Huffington Post*, "Documents Expose Huckabee's Role in Serial Rapist's Release," December 4, 2007.

205 *Arkansas Times,* "Dumond Case Revisited," September 1, 2005.

G

206 *Esquire Magazine,* July, 2003.

207 *Vanity Fair,* "The Inner Quest of Newt Gingrich,"
     September 1995; *Washington Post,* "He Knew What He
     Wanted: Gingrich Turned Disparate Lessons into Single-
     Minded Goal," December 18, 1994.

208 *Washington Post,* "Newt Gingrich, Maverick on the Hill,"
     January 3, 1985.

209 *Vanity Fair,* "The Inner Quest of Newt Gingrich,"
     September 1995.

210 *Washington Post,* "He Knew What He Wanted: Gingrich
     Turned Disparate Lessons into Single-Minded Goal,"
     December 18, 1994.

211 *Mother Jones,* "Newt Gingrich: Shining Knight of the Post-
     Reagan Right," November 1, 1984.

212 Ibid.

213 *Washington Post,* "Newt Gingrich, Maverick on the Hill,"
     January 3, 1985.

214 Ibid.

215 *Mother Jones,* "Newt Gingrich: Shining Knight of the Post-
     Reagan Right," November 1, 1984.

216 *Washington Post,* "Newt Gingrich, Maverick on the Hill,"
     January 3, 1985.

217 *Mother Jones,* "Newt Gingrich: Shining Knight of the Post-
     Reagan Right," November 1, 1984.

218 *Washington Post,* "After Political Victory, A Personal
     Revolution," December 19, 1994.

219 Ibid.

220 Ibid.

221 *Washington Post,* "Newt Gingrich, Maverick on the Hill,"
     January 3, 1985; *Mother Jones,* "Newt Gingrich: Shining
     Knight of the Post-Reagan Right," November 1, 1984.

222 *Washington Post,* "After Political Victory, A Personal
     Revolution," December 19, 1994.

223 *Mother Jones,* "Newt Gingrich: Shining Knight of the Post-Reagan Right," November 1, 1984; *Vanity Fair,* "The Inner Quest of Newt Gingrich," September 1995.

224 *Mother Jones,* "Newt Gingrich: Shining Knight of the Post-Reagan Right," November 1, 1984.

225 *Vanity Fair,* "The Inner Quest of Newt Gingrich," September 1995.

226 Ibid.

227 Ibid.

228 *Mother Jones,* "Newt Gingrich: Shining Knight of the Post-Reagan Right," November 1, 1984.

229 Ibid.

230 Ibid.

231 *Washington Post,* "After Political Victory, A Personal Revolution," December 19, 1994.

232 *Vanity Fair,* "The Inner Quest of Newt Gingrich," September 1995.

233 Ibid.

234 *Commercial Appeal* [Memphis, TN], "Newt Shrugs Off Love Affair Claims," August 11, 1995.

235 *Albuquerque Tribune,* "Gingrich 'Morally Dishonest,' Woman Says," August 10, 1995.

236 Ibid.

237 *Washington Post,* "After Political Victory, A Personal Revolution," December 19, 1994.

238 *Washington Post,* "Settled . . . But Not Over," December 18, 1999.

239 *Atlanta Journal and Constitution,* "Gingrich Wonders if Wife Had Detective Trailing Him," October 8, 1999.

240 *Vanity Fair,* "The Inner Quest of Newt Gingrich," September 1995.

241 *New York Daily News,* "Gingrich Dating, Cashing In," September 5, 1999.

242 Associated Press, "Gingrich, Aide Try to Avoid Questions about Divorce Proceedings," September 27, 1999.

243 *Atlanta Journal and Constitution,* "Gingrich Out to Annul Second Marriage," May 10, 2002.

244 *Milwaukee Journal Sentinel,* "Gingrich, Third Wife Renew Vows in Catholic Ceremony," August 8, 2003.

245 *Washington Post,* "A Lover-ly Wedding," April 10, 2005.

246 *Salon,* "Newt's Glass House," August 28, 1998.

247 ABC News Transcript, "Gingrich Admits to Affair," March 9, 2007.

248 *Honolulu Star Bulletin,* "Fox's Testimony Affirms His Sexual Misconduct," January 25, 2006.

249 Ibid.

250 *Honolulu Star Bulletin,* "Rep. Fox Quits after Sex Conviction," November 1, 2005.

251 *USA Today,* "Ex-Lawmaker Gets Probation for Airline Passenger Grope," January 26, 2006.

252 Ibid.

253 *Los Angeles Times,* "Women Say Schwarzenegger Groped, Humiliated Them," October 2, 2003.

254 *Los Angeles Times,* "Schwarzenegger Tells Backers He 'Behaved Badly,'" October 3, 2003.

255 *The Smoking Gun,* "Schwarzenegger's Sex Talk," http://www.thesmokinggun.com/archive/arnoldinter2.html (accessed March 27, 2008).

256 *Atlanta Journal and Constitution,* "Conservative Foundation's Leader Quits, Denies Charges," October 5, 2000.

257 *Atlanta Journal and Constitution,* "Glavin Given Probation in Public Indecency Case," December 15, 2000.

258 Ibid.

259 Associated Press, "Conservative Group Hurt by Charge," October 6, 2000.

260 *Deseret News,* "Legislator is Arrested, Resigns Seat," March 1, 2003.

261 Ibid.

262 *Salt Lake Tribune,* April 9, 2003.

H

263   *The O'Reilly Factor for Kids*, by Bill O'Reilly. HarperCollins, 2004. Pg. 75.

264   *Washington Post*, "Bill O'Reilly, Producer Settle Harassment Suit," October 29, 2004; *Washington Post*, "The Reliable Source," October 14, 2004.

265   Ibid.

266   *Washington Post*, "Bill O'Reilly, Producer Settle Harassment Suit," October 29, 2004.

267   *Washington Post*, "O'Reilly, Accuser Air Their Cases," October 15, 2004.

268   *Washington Post*, "The Reliable Source," October 14, 2004.

269   *Washington Post*, "Exhaustive, Damning Documents," September 8, 1995.

269a Ibid.

270   Ibid.

271   *Supreme Discomfort, The Divided Soul of Clarence Thomas*, by Kevin Merida and Michael A. Fletcher. Doubleday, 2007. Pg. 172.

272   *Hearing of the Senate Judiciary Committee on the Nomination of Clarence Thomas to the Supreme Court*, Electronic Text Center, University of Virginia Library, October 11, 1991.

273   Ibid.

274   Ibid.

275   *Supreme Discomfort, The Divided Soul of Clarence Thomas*, by Kevin Merida and Michael A. Fletcher. Doubleday, 2007. Pg. 198.

276   Ibid. Pg. 199-200.

277   *Washington Post*, "Wilkins Will Leave Va. House," July 17, 2002.

278   *Richmond Times Dispatch*, December 28, 2002.

279   Ibid.

280 *Los Angeles Times,* 1990.
281 *Washington Post,* "Clinton's Public Enemy," February 10, 1998.
282 *Slate,* "Rep. Bob Barr," February 22, 1998.
283 *Washington Post,* "Clinton's Public Enemy," February 10, 1998.
284 Ibid.
285 *American Journalism Review,* "Gatekeepers without Gates," March 1999.
286 *Salon,* "Hyde Lied, Says Former Love," September 19, 1998; Associated Press, "Rep. Hyde Admits Affair in '60s," September 17, 1998.
287 Associated Press, "Rep. Hyde Admits Affair in '60s," September 17, 1998.
288 *Salon,* "Hyde Lied, Says Former Love," September 19, 1998.
289 *Salon,* "This Hypocrite Broke Up My Family," September 16, 1998.
290 *Las Vegas Review-Journal,* "Assembly District 14," October 14, 2004.
291 Ibid.
292 *Olympian,* "Man in Notorious Sex Case Finishes Term," April 8, 2003; *Oregonian,* "Pretrial Hearing Hears Testimony of Abuse by Pair, Satanic Ritual," April 21, 1989.
293 *Olympian,* "Man in Notorious Sex Case Finishes Term," April 8, 2003.
294 *Houston Chronicle,* "Ex-Radio Host Pleads Guilty to Child Indecency," June 22, 2004.
295 Ibid.
296 Ibid.
297 *Times Leader,* "Summons Faxed to McDade's Hometown," March 29, 2007; *Times Leader,* "Cops: McDade Seen Folding Self," February 15, 2007.
298 *The Hotline,* "McDade Pleads Not Guilty with Minimal Exposure," May 2, 2007.

299   *Times Leader,* "Expert Links Meds to McDade Case," February 20, 2007.

300   Associated Press, "Veteran Legislator Charged in Florida with Indecent Exposure," June 18, 2002; *Tennessean,* "Special House Service Honors Westmoreland," June 21, 2002.

301   *Tennessean,* "Lawmaker Found Dead of Gunshot," June 20, 2002.

J

302   *Salon,* "Lives of the Republicans, Part Two," September 16, 1998.

K

303   *Florida Times-Union,* "Trinity Baptist Faces New Abuse Lawsuit," March 2, 2007.

L

304   *Times* [London], "Gingrich Advocates Victorian Values," March 15, 1995.

305   *Salon,* "Sweetheart Deal," October 5, 2004.

306   Ibid.

M

307   Investigative Sgt. Dave Karsnia #4211 and Detective Noel Nelson of the Minneapolis Police Department, Intert 1162. *Interview with Larry Craig,* Case 07002008 (June 11, 2007).

308   *Palm Beach Post,* "Allen Back at Capitol after Arrest," October 6, 2007; *CNN.com,* "McCain Campaign Official Denies Soliciting for Prostitution," July 12, 2007.

309   *Orlando Sentinel,* "Allen Explains Sex Case: Fear Made Me Play Along," August 3, 2007.

309a Ibid.

310 Ibid.

310a Ibid.

311 *MyFloridaHouse.gov*, "HB 1475: Lewd and Lascivious Exhibition Act," http://www.myfloridahouse.gov/Sections/ Bills/billsdetail.aspx?BillId=36627 (accessed March 27, 2008).

312 *Washington Post*, "GOP Senator Pleaded Guilty after Restroom Arrest," August 28, 2007; *Washington Post*, "Idaho Senator Asserts:'I Never Have Been Gay,'" August 29, 2007.

313 *Washington Post*, "GOP Senator Pleaded Guilty after Restroom Arrest," August 28, 2007.

314 *Washington Post*, "Police Release Audio of Senator's Arrest," August 31, 2007.

315 *Washington Post*, "Sen. Craig Appeals Judge's Decision," October 16, 2007.

316 *Washington Post*, "Despite Court Defeat, Craig Vows to Remain in Senate," October 5, 2007.

317 *Idaho Statesman*, "Men's Room Arrest Reopens Questions about Sen. Larry Craig," August 28, 2007.

318 Ibid.

319 *IdahoStatesman.com*, Audio Interview: More Gay Men Describe Sexual Encounters with U.S. Sen Craig, December 3, 2007, http://www.idahostatesman.com/eyepiece/ story/226703.html (accessed May 21, 2008).

320 Ibid.

321 Ibid.

322 *Idaho Statesman*, "Men's Room Arrest Reopens Questions about Sen. Larry Craig," August 28, 2007.

323 Ibid.

324 *Times-Picayune* [New Orleans, LA], "DiFatta Twice Detained for Lewd Conduct in Mall Restrooms, October 4, 2007.

325 Ibid.

326 Ibid.

327 Ibid.

N

328 *CNN.com*, "Senate Set to Reject Gay Marriage Ban," June 6, 2006.

329 NBC News Transcripts, "House Calls; Ups and Downs," November 19, 2000; *Salon*, "Tell Laura I Love Her," August 23, 1999; *Salon*, "Dr. Laura Targets the New Sodom: Librarians," May 27, 1999.

330 NBC News Transcripts, "House Calls; Ups and Downs," November 19, 2000; *Salon*, "Tell Laura I Love Her," August 23, 1999.

331 *Hartford Courant*, "Listeners, Other Hosts Support Dr. Laura," November 7, 1998.

332 NBC News Transcripts, "House Calls; Ups and Downs," November 19, 2000.

O

333 *Detroit Free Press*, "Federal Prosecutor Is Arrested in Sex Sting," September 18, 2007.

P

334 Congressional Press Releases, "Foley, Hatch Announce Sweeping Overhaul of Sex Offender Laws," May 18, 2005.

335 United Press International, "Crane Supports Own Censure," July 20, 1983.

336 Ibid.

337 *Washington Post*, "House Censures Crane and Studds," July 21, 1983.

338 *Washington Post*, "The Open and Closeted Lives of Gay Congressman," October 4, 2006.

339 Ibid.

340 *Washington Post*, "Foley Lawyer Cites Alcohol, Childhood Abuse," October 4, 2006.

341   Ibid.

342   *Marine Corps Times,* "Corps May Investigate CPL's Gay Porn Past," March 16, 2007.

343   *Advocate,* "Matt Sanchez: I'm Bad at Being Gay," March 8, 2007.

344   *Denver Post,* "Records, Porn Seized from Home," December 16, 2001.

345   *Rocky Mountain News* [Denver, CO], "From Politics to Porn Flicks," August 7, 2004.

346   Ibid.

347   *Press Enterprise* [Riverside, CA], "Closing the Door in '94," January 1, 1995.

348   *Roll Call,* "California: Calvert Scandal Detailed in Police Report," April 26, 1994.

349   *Press Enterprise,* "Closing the Door in '94," January 1, 1995.

350   *Press-Enterprise,* "Rep. Calvert Started to Flee from Police," April 23, 1994.

351   *Project Vote Smart,* "Family Research Council," http://www.votesmart.org/issue_rating_detail.php?r_id=3553 (accessed March 27, 2008).

352   *Press Enterprise,* "Calvert's Ex-Wife Drops Restraining Order Request," October 18, 1996.

353   *Press Enterprise,* "Clavert Sues in Alimony Row with Ex," October 7, 1996.

354   Spokane Police Report, Case No: 07-808376, October 27, 2007.

355   Ibid.

356   Ibid.; *The Stranger,* "Straight Acting," November 7, 2007.

357   *The Stranger,* "Straight Acting," November 7, 2007; *King5. com,* "Rep. Richard Curtis Resigns Over Gay Scandal," October 31, 2007.

358   *Press Enterprise,* "Spotlight: Man Tells about His Relationship with the Rev. Ted Haggard," September 30, 2007.

359   Ibid.

360   *USA Today*, "Minister: Haggard Completely Heterosexual," February 6, 2007; *Rocky Mountain News*, "More Allegations for Ted Haggard," February 19, 2007; *Denver Post*, "Haggard Says He is Completely Heterosexual," December 24, 2007.

361   *Press Enterprise*, "Spotlight: Man Tells about His Relationship with the Rev. Ted Haggard," September 30, 2007.

362   *Gazette* [Colorado Springs, CO], "Pastor Says Haggard Won't Work in Ariz. Halfway House," August 28, 2007.

363   Ibid.

364   Ibid.

365   Ibid.

366   *Advocate* [Baton Rouge, LA], "Vitter Apologizes, Sets Sights on Work," July 17, 2007.

367   Ibid.

368   Ibid.

369   *Times-Picayune*, "Madam Has Vitter in Mind for Witness List," July 19, 2007.

370   Docket Sheet, *USA v. Palfrey*, United States District Court District of Columbia, Case No. 07-cr-00046, October 16, 2007.

371   *Times-Picayune*, "Ex-Call Girl, Flynt Keep Pressure on Vitter," September 12, 2007; *Advocate*, "Vitter Takes Another Hit," September 15, 2007.

372   *Washington Post*, "Sculpted Bodies and a Strip Act at Justice Dept.," June 25, 2005.

373   *BBCNEWS.com*, "Curtains for Semi-Nude Justice Statue," January 29, 2002.

Q

374   *Washington Post*, "After Political Victory, A Personal Revolution," December 19, 1994.

R

375   *Today Show*, NBC, March 11, 2008.

376   *Washington Post*, "Sex and Cash Scandal Rock Montana Town," April 15, 2004.

377   *Time*, "DC Madam: Suicide before Prison," May 1, 2008.

378 Associated Press, "Supco: Search in Prostitution Case Was Legal," April 4, 2007.
379 *Washington Post*, "Sex and Cash Scandal Rock Montana Town," April 15, 2004.
380 Associated Press, "Former Legislator Pleads Not Guilty," July 11, 2007.
381 Associated Press, "Another Court Hearing in the Ted Klaudt Case," October 20, 2007.
382 Associated Press, "Foster Daughter Sues Former S.D. State Lawmaker Who Raped Her and Another Girl," March 11, 2008.
383 *Keloland TV*, "Klaudt's Legislative Record," March 18, 2007.
384 Associated Press & Local Wire, "Klaudt's Lawyers: Dismiss Lawsuit or Move It," April 2, 2008.
385 Associated Press, "New Evidence Surfaces against Former Lawmaker," August 7, 2007.
386 *Lancaster New Era*, "Wrightsville Official Charged in Teen's Rape," September 2, 2004.
387 *Intelligencer Journal*, [Lancaster, PA], "Sex Crimes Figure in Wrightsville Mayor Race," October 28, 2005.
388 *Virginian-Pilot*, "Convicted Sex Offender Nearly Wins GOP Award," February 13, 2002.
389 Ibid.

S

390 *The Nation*, "Dr. Hager's Family Values," May 30, 2005.
391 *Time*, "Was It for Love or Money?" October 4, 1982; *Crime Library*, Courtroom Television Network, 2007.
392 Ibid.
393 Ibid.
394 Ibid.
395 *Chicago Tribune*, "Ryan's Ruin: He Figured All the Angles Save One," June 27, 2004.
396 *Ryan v. Ryan* BD. 290 382 (Los Angeles Superior Court, 2000).
397 *Chicago Tribune*, "Ryan Aide to Give Obama More Space," May 23, 2004.

398 *Washington Post,* "The Relatively Charmed Life of Neil Bush," December 28, 2003.

399 Ibid.

400 Ibid.

401 *Des Moines Register,* "President Trumpets Tax-Break Extensions," October 5, 2004.

402 Ibid.

403 *Omaha World-Herald,* "Youth Pastor is Charged in Affair with Girl," December 9, 2004; Associated Press, "Youth Pastor Pleads Guilty to Sexual Exploitation by a Counselor," March 8, 2005.

404 Associated Press, "Youth Pastor Pleads Guilty to Sexual Exploitation by a Counselor," March 8, 2005.

405 *Lexington Herald Leader,* "A Physician and a Lightening Rod," June 12, 2005.

406 *Lexington Herald Leader,* "Gynecologist Expects to be Off Panel," May 13, 2005.

407 *The Nation,* "Dr. Hager's Family Values," May 30, 2005.

408 *Lexington Herald Leader,* "Gynecologist Expects to be Off Panel," May 13, 2005.

409 *Lexington Herald Leader,* "A Physician and a Lightening Rod," June 12, 2005.

410 *The Nation,* "Dr. Hager's Family Values," May 30, 2005.

411 *St. Louis Post-Dispatch,* "GOP Committeeman is Charged with Having Sex with Teen Boy," December 7, 2002.

412 Associated Press, "Man Found Innocent of Underage Sex Charges," August 26, 2004.

413 Ibid.; *St. Louis Post-Dispatch,* "GOP Committeeman is Charged with Having Sex with Teen Boy," December 7, 2002.

414 Associated Press, "Man Found Innocent of Underage Sex Charges," August 26, 2004.

415 *Detroit Free Press,* "Federal Prosecutor is Arrested in Sex Sting," September 18, 2007.

416 Ibid.

417 *Detroit News,* "Prosecutor in Sex Sting Hung Himself in Shower, Autopsy Shows," October 9, 2007; *Detroit News,* "Few Details Released after Federal Prosecutor's Suicide in Milan," October 7, 2007.

418   *The Hill*, "Bob Bauman Wants to Testify before Subcommittee on Educational Programs," November 29, 1995; *St. Petersburg Times*, "Long after the Fall, Ex-Capitol Star Still Struggles," January 18, 1993.

419   Ibid.

420   *St. Petersburg Times*, "Long after the Fall, Ex-Capitol Star Still Struggles," January 18, 1993.

421   Ibid.

422   Ibid.

423   Ibid.

424   *The Hill*, "Bob Bauman Wants to Testify before Subcommittee on Educational Programs," November 29, 1995.

425   *St. Louis Post-Dispatch*, "Prosecutor Defends Sentence in Sex Case," January 11, 2005.

426   Ibid.

427   *Post-Standard* [Syracuse, NY], "FBI: Mayor Offered Drugs, Cash for Sex with Minors," September 18, 2005.

428   *Post-Standard*, "Oswego Mayor Gets Curfew," September 18, 2005

429   *Post-Standard*, "Former Oswego Mayor Indicted on Two Counts," November 4, 2005.

430   *Post-Standard*, "Gosek Starts Three-Year Sentence in N.C. Prison," August 30, 2006; *Post-Standard*, "Gosek Gets 37 Months," July 19, 2006.

431   *Post-Standard*, "I Never Expected the Underage Girls to be at the Hotel," July 23, 2006.

432   *Post-Standard*, "FBI: Mayor Offered Drugs, Cash for Sex with Minors," September 18, 2005.

433   *Post-Standard*, "I Never Expected the Underage Girls to be at the Hotel," July 23, 2006.

434   *Post-Standard*, "Ex-Mayor's Spending: From Hotel to Hooters," December 28, 2005.

435   *Virginian-Pilot*, "Former Law Student Sentenced to 7 Years," July 27, 2004; *Virginian-Pilot*, "Ex-Law Student Convicted of Sex Crimes," April 23, 2004.

436   Ibid.

437   *Washington Post*, "Consultants for Va. Candidate Linked to Indicted Lobbyist," November 3, 2005.

438 *Philadelphia Inquirer*, "Preacher Convicted in Sex Case," January 15, 2004; *Philadelphia Inquirer*, "Preacher Is Jailed on Sex Charges," March 20, 2004.

439 Ibid.

440 *Philadelphia Inquirer*, "Preacher Convicted in Sex Case," January 15, 2004.

441 Ibid.

442 *Portland Press Herald*, "Hathaway Looks at Run for Governor," January 29, 2002; *Bangor Daily News*, "Hathaway Denies Sex Allegations," June 6, 1996.

443 *Bangor Daily News*, "Hathaway Denies Sex Allegations," June 6, 1996.

444 Ibid.

445 *Portland Press Herald*, "Hathaway Looks at Run for Governor," January 29, 2002.

446 *New York Daily News*, "Sex Flap Hits GOPer," September 13, 1996.

447 Ibid.

448 Ibid.

T

449 *Sydney Morning Herald*, "We Better Learn What Makes Newt Run," December 9, 1994.

450 *Daily Press*, "Schrock Votes to Ban Gay Marriage," October 1, 2004; *Virginian-Pilot*, "For Now, Rep. Ed Schrock Turns Focus to His Family," September 10, 2004; *Raw Story*, "Rep. Schrock Resigns after 'Gay Phone Sex Call,' Surfaces on Web," August 31, 2004.

451 *Gay Peoples Chronicle*, "House Member Won't Seek Re-election after Being Outed," September 3, 2004.

452 Associated Press, "Republican Rep. Ed Schrock of Virginia Announces His Retirement Following Allegations He Is Gay," August 31, 2004.

453 *Virginian-Pilot*, October 22, 2000.

454 United Press International, "Scandal-Tainted GOPer Gets Job in Congress," December 17, 2004.

U

455 *New York Times,* "Word for Word/Online Animus; Talking Back to Talk Radio: Dr. Laura Attracts a Crowd," July 30, 2000.

456 *Democratic Underground,* "Top 10 Conservative Idiots," http://www.democraticunderground.com/top10/01/ top10_2001_15.html (accessed March 31, 2008).

457 *The Brotherhood of the Disappearing Pants,* by Joseph Minton Amann and Tom Breuer. Nation Books, 2007. Pg. 204–06.

458 Associated Press, "Clark County GOP Chairman Quits Amid Investigation," August 8, 2007.

459 Ibid.

460 Ibid.; *Evening News,* "Glenn Murphy Jr. Charged with Class B Felony," November 9, 2007.

461 *News and Tribune,* "Glenn Murphy Jr. Moving Toward Trial," April 7, 2008.

V

462 *Salon,* "Portrait of a Political 'Pit Bull,'" September 13, 1995.

W

463 *New York Post,* "'Pop' Goes the Weasel," May 9, 2008; *New York Times,* "Mother's Day Scandal," May 10, 2008.

464 *New York Daily News,* "Romance and Ruins," May 11, 2008.

465 *New York Post,* "Mother Lode of Sleazebaggery," May 13, 2008.

466 *New York Post,* "'Pop' Goes the Weasel," May 9, 2008.

467 *New York Post,* "Mother Lode of Sleazebaggery," May 13, 2008.

468 *New York Times,* "Woman, 78, Says She Is Daughter of Thurmond," December 14, 2003.

469 *FOXNews.com,* "Thurmond Holds Senate Record for Filibustering," June 27, 2003.

470 *CBSNews.com,* "Essie Mae on Strom Thurmond," December 17, 2003.

X

471   *DemocraticUnderground.com*, "Top 10 Conservative Idiots," April 23, 2001. http://www.democraticunderground.com/ top 10/01/top10_2001_15.html (accessed March 31, 2008).

Y

472   *New York Times*, "The Sidney Awards," December 25, 2007.

Z

473   Jerry Falwell, interviewed by Pat Robertson, *The 700 Club*, CBN, September 13, 2001.

APPENDIX A

SUPREME COURT OF THE STATE OF NEW YORK
COUNTY OF NEW YORK
===============================X
ANDREA MACKRIS,

    Plaintiff,

       -against-

BILL O'REILLY, NEWS CORPORATION,
FOX NEWS CHANNEL, TWENTIETH
CENTURY FOX FILM CORP., and
WESTWOOD ONE, INC.,

    Defendants.

===============================X

**VERIFIED
COMPLAINT**

Index No.:   **04114558**

FILED

OCT 13 2004

NEW YORK
COUNTY CLERK'S OFF

Plaintiff ANDREA MACKRIS, by her attorneys, BENEDICT P. MORELLI &

ASSOCIATES, P.C., complaining of the Defendants herein, upon information and belief

respectfully alleges as follows:

    1.   Plaintiff **ANDREA MACKRIS** is a resident of the City, County and State of

New York.

    2.   Plaintiff **ANDREA MACKRIS**, a graduate of the Columbia School of Journalism,

is a highly driven and successful journalist whose television news production career has included

stints at NBC, CNN and Fox. In 1991, Plaintiff served as an intern in George Bush's White

House. Throughout her career, Plaintiff **ANDREA MACKRIS** has been praised for her

proficiency, dedication and skill.

    3.   At all times mentioned herein, Defendant NEWS CORPORATION, was and is

a corporation incorporated in Delaware with its principal place of business in New York.

Defendant NEWS CORPORATION is one of the largest media corporations in the world.

4.   At all times mentioned herein, Defendant FOX NEWS CHANNEL was and is a corporation incorporated in Delaware with its principal place of business in New York.

5.   At all times mentioned herein, Defendant FOX NEWS CHANNEL was and is the wholly-owned subsidiary of Defendant NEWS CORPORATION.

6.   At all times mentioned herein, Defendant TWENTIETH CENTURY FOX FILM CORP. was and is a corporation incorporated in Delaware with its principal place of business in New York. Defendant TWENTIETH CENTURY FOX FILM CORP. produces, acquires and distributes big-budget motion pictures.

7.   At all times mentioned herein, Defendant TWENTIETH CENTURY FOX FILM CORP. was and is the wholly-owned subsidiary of Defendant NEWS CORPORATION.

8.   Hereinafter, Defendants FOX NEWS CHANNEL FOX , TWENTIETH CENTURY FOX FILM CORP. and NEWS CORPORATION shall be designated collectively as Defendants "FOX."

9.   At all times mentioned herein, Defendant WESTWOOD ONE, INC. was and is a corporation incorporated in Delaware with its principal place of business in New York. Defendant WESTWOOD ONE, INC. ("WESTWOOD ONE") is one of the largest producers and distributors of radio programming in the United States.

10.   At all times mentioned herein, Defendant BILL O'REILLY has held himself out as a morally upright, independent political pundit.

11.   At all times mentioned herein, Defendant BILL O'REILLY was and is the host and "star" of "The O'Reilly Factor." "The O'Reilly Factor" is broadcast on cable television throughout the United States by Defendants FOX. "The O'Reilly Factor" is broadcast on radio throughout the United States by Defendant WESTWOOD ONE. Defendants FOX,

WESTWOOD ONE and BILL O'REILLY utilize this forum to preach the principles of the so-called "compassionate conservatism" espoused by George W. Bush and the Republican Party. The Defendants also use this forum to preach their belief in family values and to bemoan the moral decline of politicians and others in positions of power.

12.   As of the week of September 20, 2004, "The O'Reilly Factor" ranked among the top ten most popular cable television broadcasts in the United States. "The O'Reilly Factor" generates approximately $60,000,000.00 annual revenue for Defendants.

13.   During the period from on or about April 2000 through on or about January 2004, and again during the period from on or about July 6, 2004 through the present, Plaintiff ANDREA MACKRIS was and is now employed by Defendants FOX.

14.   During the period from on or about July 6, 2004 through the present, Plaintiff ANDREA MACKRIS was and is now also employed by Defendant WESTWOOD ONE.

15.   From on or about April 2000 through or about January 2004, and commencing again on or about July 6, 2004 through the present, Plaintiff ANDREA MACKRIS was and continues to be employed by Defendants FOX as an "Associate Producer" for "The O'Reilly Factor."

16.   Commencing on or about July 6, 2004 through the present, Plaintiff ANDREA MACKRIS was and continues to be employed by Defendants FOX and Defendant WESTWOOD ONE a staff member of "The O'Reilly Factor."

17.   Throughout Plaintiff's employment at FOX, Rupert Murdoch was and continues to be Chief Executive Officer, the highest ranking supervisor, an officer, manager and employee of Defendants FOX.

18.   Throughout Plaintiff's employment at FOX, Roger Ailes was and continues

to be President, the highest ranking supervisor of Fox News Channel, an officer, manager and employee of Defendants FOX. At all times mentioned herein, President Roger Ailes was and continues to be supervised by Chief Executive Officer Rupert Murdoch.

19.   Throughout Plaintiff's employment at FOX, Defendant BILL O'REILLY was and continues to be the "star" of "The O'Reilly Factor," Plaintiff's immediate supervisor, and a manager and employee of Defendants FOX. At all times mentioned herein, Defendant BILL O'REILLY was and continues to be supervised by FOX President Roger Ailes.

20.   Throughout her employment at Defendant FOX, Plaintiff ANDREA MACKRIS has reported directly to, and been supervised by, Defendant BILL O'REILLY.

21.   Throughout Plaintiff's employment at WESTWOOD ONE, Defendant BILL O'REILLY was and continues to be the "star" of "The O'Reilly Factor," Plaintiff's immediate supervisor, and a manager and employee of Defendants WESTWOOD ONE.

22.   Throughout her employment at Defendant WESTWOOD ONE, Plaintiff ANDREA MACKRIS has reported directly to, and been supervised by, Defendant BILL O'REILLY.

23.   At all times material to this Complaint, the individual officers, directors, supervisors, managers, employees and/or agents mentioned herein, acted within the scope of their duties as officers, directors, supervisors, managers, employees and/or agents of Defendants FOX and/or WESTWOOD ONE.

ALLEGATIONS OF QUID PRO QUO SEXUAL HARASSMENT AND A SEXUALLY HOSTILE WORK ENVIRONMENT

24.   Throughout her employment at Defendants FOX, commencing approximately May 2002 through January 2004, and commencing again approximately July 6, 2004 through the

present, Plaintiff **ANDREA MACKRIS** has been subjected to *quid pro quo* sexual harassment at the hands of her immediate supervisor, Defendant **BILL O'REILLY**, and a sexually hostile work environment, perpetrated by Defendant **BILL O'REILLY**, and other supervisors, managers, officers, employees and/or agents of Defendants **FOX**.

25. Throughout her employment at Defendant **WESTWOOD ONE**, commencing approximately July 6, 2004 through the present, Plaintiff **ANDREA MACKRIS** has been subjected to *quid pro quo* sexual harassment at the hands of her immediate supervisor, Defendant **BILL O'REILLY**, and a sexually hostile work environment, perpetrated by Defendant **BILL O'REILLY**, and other supervisors, managers, officers, employees and/or agents of Defendant **WESTWOOD ONE**.

26. Within Defendants **FOX** and **WESTWOOD ONE** a permissive and encouraging environment for gender discrimination and sexual harassment reigns among supervisors, managers and employees of the companies

27. During the period from approximately May 2002 through January 2004, and commencing again approximately July 6, 2004 through the present, extending prior to and subsequent to those dates, Defendants **BILL O'REILLY** and **FOX**, its employees, managers, directors, officers and agents, harassed and intimidated Plaintiff, and created and maintained a virulently hostile work environment through explicit, rampant, pervasive and continued sex discrimination and sexual harassment against Plaintiff **ANDREA MACKRIS** and other female employees that was so offensive and severe that it detrimentally altered the terms and conditions of Plaintiff's employment.

28. During the period from approximately July 6, 2004 through the present, extending prior to and subsequent to those dates, Defendants **BILL O'REILLY** and **WESTWOOD ONE**,

its employees, managers, directors, officers and agents, harassed and intimidated Plaintiff, and created and maintained a virulently hostile work environment through explicit, rampant, pervasive and continued sex discrimination and sexual harassment against Plaintiff ANDREA MACKRIS and other female employees that was so offensive and severe that it detrimentally altered the terms and conditions of Plaintiff's employment.

29.   Throughout her employment on "The O'Reilly Factor" Plaintiff ANDREA MACKRIS has found her work challenging and engaging. Indeed, her career as an Associate Producer at FOX and a staff member at WESTWOOD ONE has involved precisely the type of work that she studied and prepared for her entire adult life.

30.   However, throughout her employment on "The O'Reilly Factor," Plaintiff ANDREA MACKRIS has been subjected to the mercurial and unpredictable mood swings of her boss, Defendant "BILL O'REILLY," a personality who can be paternal and engaging at one instant, tyrannical and menacing the next.

31.   Commencing approximately May 2002 through January 2004, and commencing again approximately July 6, 2004 through the present, Plaintiff ANDREA MACKRIS was sexually harassed by her immediate supervisor, Defendant BILL O'REILLY.

32.   On or about May 1, 2002, Plaintiff ANDREA MACKRIS informed Vice President Bill Shine of the break-up of her long-term relationship with her fiancé. During the course of that conversation, Plaintiff informed Mr. Shine that she would no longer be able to afford to work at Defendants FOX on her approximately $56,000 salary.

33.   Shortly thereafter, in or about early May 2002, Plaintiff's supervisor, Defendant BILL O'REILLY, invited Plaintiff ANDREA MACKRIS out to dinner, purportedly to discuss

her future at FOX. During the course of their conversation, Defendant **BILL O'REILLY** praised Plaintiff's skill as a Booker, told Plaintiff he could not afford to lose her from his production team, and promptly raised her salary to $65,000.

34.   During the course of this dinner in approximately early May 2002, Plaintiff's supervisor, Defendant **BILL O'REILLY**, lavished Plaintiff **ANDREA MACKRIS** with unsolicited advice regarding her handling of future relationships with members of the opposite sex. Defendant **BILL O'REILLY** advised Plaintiff **ANDREA MACKRIS** to avoid future contact with her ex-fiancé, to have manicures and pedicures and "pick up 23-year-old men in bars," to attend charity events and meet men with credentials, and to otherwise spend the next year doing what she felt like doing, without thinking twice about the consequences. Defendant **BILL O'REILLY** then suggested that at the end of the year, they'd discuss promoting Plaintiff to a producer position for "The O'Reilly Factor."

35.   After these words during the course of their dinner in early May 2002, Defendant **BILL O'REILLY's** demeanor abruptly changed. O'REILLY's eyes became glazed and bizarrely strayed in opposite directions. Suddenly, without provocation or warning, Defendant **BILL O'REILLY** said to Plaintiff **ANDREA MACKRIS**: "And just use your vibrator to blow off steam." When Plaintiff reddened, Defendant **BILL O'REILLY** asked lewdly: "What, you've got a vibrator, don't you? Every girl does." When Plaintiff responded indignantly, "No, and no, they don't. Does your wife?" Defendant replied: "Yes, in fact she does. She'd kill me if she knew I was telling you!" Plaintiff was repulsed.

36.   During the course of their dinner in early May 2002, Defendant **BILL O'REILLY** proceeded, without solicitation or invite, to inform Plaintiff **ANDREA MACKRIS** that he had advised another woman to purchase a vibrator, and had taught that woman how to masturbate

while telling her sexual stories over the telephone. O'REILLY told Plaintiff ANDREA MACKRIS she knew the woman from FOX. Defendant O'REILLY then boasted that the woman had her first orgasm via masturbation as he spoke to her on the telephone.

37.   When Plaintiff responded that she never engaged in phone sex, Defendant BILL O'REILLY professed disbelief, and told her that the sexual stories he told were all based upon his own experiences, such as when he received a massage in a cabana in Bali and the "little short brown woman" asked to see his penis and was "amazed." Defendant BILL O'REILLY then suggested that he tell Plaintiff the same sexual stories, which he knew she would "just love." Shocked and embarrassed, Plaintiff ANDREA MACKRIS informed Defendant in no uncertain terms that she was neither experienced in nor interested in gaining experience in telephone sex. Defendant expressed disbelief.

38.   As they left the restaurant next to Defendant's hotel, Plaintiff ANDREA MACKRIS thanked her boss for the dinner and raise. Defendant BILL O'REILLY responded suggestively: "Stick with me and I'll take care of you," winked, and walked into his hotel.

39.   On or about March 9-13, 2003, Defendant BILL O'REILLY, Plaintiff ANDREA MACKRIS and other FOX employees traveled with "The O'Reilly Factor" to tape in Los Angeles. At approximately 10:30 p.m. one of those evenings, O'REILLY called Plaintiff on her cell phone. Plaintiff was at dinner with a woman friend from college. Defendant was flirtatious, repeatedly asking Plaintiff what she and her friend were wearing.

40.   Later during that week, on or about March 9-13, 2003, Defendant BILL O'REILLY joined Plaintiff ANDREA MACKRIS and other staff members at the Peninsula Hotel for cocktails. Plaintiff ANDREA MACKRIS' college friend was with her. O'REILLY approached the two and commented: "University of Missouri... Boy, I would've had fun with you

two" and alluded to having a menage a trois with Plaintiff and her friend.

41.   On or about May 2003, Defendant BILL O'REILLY took Plaintiff ANDREA MACKRIS and her college friend to dinner at Da Silvano's. During the course of the dinner, O'REILLY repeatedly propositioned the women, singing the praises of telephone sex, offering to telephone them both, and suggesting that the three of them "go to a hotel together and have the time of [their] lives." O'REILLY further suggested that the women needed to be trained so they'd be equipped and ready to go when a "real man shows up in your lives," and offered "lessons." O'REILLY further suggested they use their sexuality to their advantage so they'd have power over men, otherwise men would have power over them. Plaintiff was extremely embarrassed and protested: "Bill, you're my boss!"

42.   During the course of this dinner, in approximately May 2003, Defendant BILL O'REILLY, without solicitation or invite, regaled Plaintiff and her friend with stories concerning the loss of his virginity to a girl in a car at JFK, two "really wild" Scandinavian airline stewardesses he had gotten together with, and a "girl" at a sex show in Thailand who had shown him things in a backroom that "blew [his] mind." Defendant then stated he was going to Italy to meet the Pope, that his pregnant wife was staying at home with his daughter, and implied he was looking forward to some extra-marital dalliances with the "hot" Italian women. Both Plaintiff and her friend were repulsed, but felt powerless to protest strongly since Defendant was Plaintiff's boss and a powerful man at FOX. Defendant finally stopped after noting: "MACKRIS can't handle it."

43.   On or about September 2003, Defendant BILL O'REILLY asked Plaintiff ANDREA MACKRIS to dinner at an Italian restaurant around the corner from FOX, purportedly to discuss business. During the course of dinner, Defendant once again raised the

specter of telephone sex, repeatedly professing disbelief that Plaintiff had never engaged in telephone sex. Defendant O'REILLY repeatedly begged Plaintiff to have telephone sex with him that night. Plaintiff refused.

44.   In approximately early December 2003, Defendant BILL O'REILLY noted that Plaintiff ANDREA MACKRIS had endured a hard day at work, and took her to dinner at the Italian restaurant around the corner. Plaintiff informed Defendant that CNN had been recruiting her for a position. Defendant attempted to persuade Plaintiff not to leave FOX.

45.   During that same dinner in approximately December 2003, Defendant BILL O'REILLY once again tried to convince Plaintiff ANDREA MACKRIS to engage in telephone sex with him. Plaintiff again adamantly refused, becoming extremely embarrassed and reminding O'REILLY that he was her boss.

46.   During the course of this dinner, Defendant BILL O'REILLY bragged that he had telephone sex with other young women.

47.   On or about January 2004, Plaintiff ANDREA MACKRIS left Defendants FOX and "The O'Reilly Factor" for a position with CNN.

48.   On or about mid-February 2004, Defendant BILL O'REILLY announced to the staff of his show that by leaving "The O'Reilly Factor" for CNN, Plaintiff ANDREA MACKRIS had committed "career suicide."

49.   On or about early March 2004, Defendant BILL O'REILLY telephoned Plaintiff ANDREA MACKRIS and promised, "If anything bad happens to you at CNN, I'll get you a job."

50.   On or about March 16, 2004, Defendant BILL O'REILLY telephoned Plaintiff at

home, purportedly with advice as to how to handle office politics at CNN.

51. On or about March 21, 2004, Defendant **BILL O'REILLY** telephoned Plaintiff **ANDREA MACKRIS** again at home.

52. On or about early April 2004, Defendant **BILL O'REILLY** left a message on Plaintiff's answering machine at home after her boss at CNN was terminated for sexual harassment, purportedly to determine if anything untoward was directed toward her. **O'REILLY** suggested they go to dinner to discuss her future, as Plaintiff had previously expressed unhappiness with her position at CNN.

53. On or about early April 2004, Defendant **BILL O'REILLY** telephoned Plaintiff at home. Plaintiff **ANDREA MACKRIS** then told Defendant that she would only have dinner with him if the talk was professional. Defendant **BILL O'REILLY** agreed.

54. On or about April 13, 2004, during dinner at Milos, Plaintiff **ANDREA MACKRIS** again told Defendant **BILL O'REILLY** that she would return to work on "The O'Reilly Factor" only if he no longer engaged in inappropriate conduct. Defendant agreed: "Of course, because then you'd be working for me and I'd have power over you, so that couldn't happen, that wouldn't be fair." When Plaintiff reminded Defendant that he had done the same thing to other women who worked on "The O'Reilly Factor," and that he should be careful or they might tell someone, **O'REILLY** vehemently threatened with words to the effect:

> If any woman ever breathed a word I'll make her pay so
> dearly that she'll wish she'd never been born. I'll rake her
> through the mud, bring up things in her life and make her
> so miserable that she'll be destroyed. And besides, she wouldn't
> be able to afford the lawyers I can or endure it financially as long
> as I can. And nobody would believe her, it'd be her word against
> mine and who are they going to believe? Me or some unstable
> woman making outrageous accusations. They'd see her as some psycho,
> someone unstable. Besides, I'd never make the mistake of picking

unstable crazy girls like that.

 55.   During the course of this conversation, Defendant **BILL O'REILLY** further sternly warned, to the effect:

> If you cross **FOX NEWS CHANNEL**, it's not just me,
> it's [FOX President] Roger Ailes who will go after you.
> I'm the street guy out front making loud noises about
> the issues, but Ailes operates behind the scenes,
> strategizes and makes things happen so that one day BAM!
> The person gets what's coming to them but never sees it
> coming. Look at Al Franken, one day he's going to get a
> knock on his door and life as he's known it will change forever.
> That day will happen, trust me.

56.   During the course of this conversation, Defendant **BILL O'REILLY** bizarrely rambled further about Al Franken: "Ailes knows very powerful people and this goes all the way to the top." Plaintiff queried: "To the top of what?" Defendant responded: "Top of the country. Just look at who's on the cover of his book [Bush and Cheney], they're watching him and will be for years. [Al Franken's] finished, and he's going to be sorry he ever took **FOX NEWS CHANNEL** on." Plaintiff found O'REILLY's paranoid rambling both strange and alarming.

57.   On or about April 13, 2004, during dinner, Defendant **BILL O'REILLY** and Plaintiff **ANDREA MACKRIS** discussed the possibility of her returning to Defendants FOX and working on "The O'Reilly Factor."

58.   At the conclusion of their dinner on April 13, 2004, Defendant **BILL O'REILLY** asked Plaintiff **ANDREA MACKRIS** to come watch the President's press conference on the television in his hotel room. They watched the press conference without incident. Plaintiff ridiculed President Bush, O'REILLY laughed, and decided which highlight he would focus upon during his show the next day.

59.   On or about June 4, 2004, following the departure of yet another female Producer from "The O'Reilly Factor," Defendant **BILL O'REILLY** and Plaintiff **ANDREA MACKRIS** again discussed the possibility of her returning to FOX to work on the show. Plaintiff stated she would be willing to return to FOX if FOX matched her salary at CNN.

60.   On or about June 7, 2004, Defendant **BILL O'REILLY** telephoned Plaintiff **ANDREA MACKRIS** and offered her her former position at the same salary she was earning at CNN. Plaintiff accepted the offer and thanked him. Defendant **BILL O'REILLY** told Plaintiff: "You can thank me by taking me out to dinner."

61.   On or about June 8, 2004, Defendant **BILL O'REILLY** confessed to Plaintiff **ANDREA MACKRIS** that Roger Ailes had refused to match her salary at CNN and that Defendants FOX would only pay her former salary of $73,000. However, Defendant **BILL O'REILLY** assured Plaintiff that he would also pay her to serve as a staff member of his radio show, distributed by Defendant **WESTWOOD ONE**, to make up the difference.

62.   On or about July 6, 2004, Plaintiff **ANDREA MACKRIS** returned to her position as Associate Producer of "The O'Reilly Factor" at the **FOX NEWS CHANNEL**, and simultaneously commenced her position as a staff member of "The O'Reilly Factor" for Defendant **WESTWOOD ONE**.

63.   Upon her return to Defendants FOX, Plaintiff expressed her interest in covering one or both of the political conventions to Defendant **BILL O'REILLY**. **O'REILLY** indicated it was too late for her to be given those assignments.

64.   Throughout July and August 2004, Defendant **BILL O'REILLY** repeatedly reminded Plaintiff that she "owed" him dinner.

65.   On or about August 2, 2004, Defendant **BILL O'REILLY** telephoned Plaintiff

ANDREA MACKRIS at her home after interviewing two porn stars on "The O'Reilly Factor." Apparently, O'REILLY was "excited" from the show. With little preamble, Defendant BILL O'REILLY launched into a vile and degrading monologue about sex.

▶ 66. During the course of O'REILLY's telephone monologue on August 2, 2004, he suggested that Plaintiff ANDREA MACKRIS purchase a vibrator and name it, and that he had one "shaped like a cock with a little battery in it" that a woman had given him. It became apparent that Defendant was masturbating as he spoke. After he climaxed, Defendant O'REILLY said to Plaintiff: "I appreciate the fun phone call. You can have fun tonight. I'll appreciate it. I mean it." Plaintiff felt as if the floor had fallen out from beneath her. She was shocked, frightened and upset. She felt trapped.

67. On or about August 15, 2004, Defendant BILL O'REILLY telephoned Plaintiff ANDREA MACKRIS at her home. Plaintiff did not answer.

68. At approximately 10:20 p.m. on or about August 17, 2004, Defendant BILL O'REILLY called Plaintiff's home phone and left a message on her answering machine asking that she return his call on his cell phone.

69. On or about August 18, 2004, concerned that his call was work-related, Plaintiff ANDREA MACKRIS returned her boss' telephone call and left a message that she was returning his call.

70. At approximately 9:25 p.m. on or about August 19, 2004, Defendant BILL O'REILLY telephoned Plaintiff ANDREA MACKRIS again at home. Again, Plaintiff decided not to answer the phone. Defendant left a message indicating that he would like to go out for the dinner "owed" him on August 24, 2004.

71. On or about August 24, 2004, Defendant BILL O'REILLY and Plaintiff

ANDREA MACKRIS went to dinner at Periyal. O'REILLY informed Plaintiff that both he and "The O'Reilly Factor" were really hurt when she left Defendants FOX for CNN, that it's made a big difference to have her back, that "the second floor," (alluding to FOX management) liked her, and that: "You have a bright career ahead of you."

72.   During the course of this conversation, on or about August 24, 2004, Defendant BILL O'REILLY again started talking about sex, and suggested that if he had a hotel room that night he would have invited her up. Defendant further suggested that Plaintiff ANDREA MACKRIS purchase a vibrator. When Plaintiff became embarrassed and told him that she was not interested, O'REILLY again suggested: "We should do it together, I could coach you through it." Plaintiff declined.

73.   During the course of this conversation, on or about August 24, 2004, Defendant BILL O'REILLY further indicated that "the second floor," (i.e., FOX management) considered a woman producer to be "psychotic" and that she was "as far as she'll ever go at FOX."

74.   On or about August 26, 2004, within two days of their dinner, Plaintiff ANDREA MACKRIS learned that she had been assigned to attend the Republican National Convention, and that she was the only staffer attending the convention with full access passes to the booth and floor.

75.   On or about August 26, 2004, within two days of their dinner, Plaintiff ANDREA MACKRIS learned that she would be interviewing Senator Hillary Clinton on August 29, 2004 for "The O'Reilly Factor."

76.   At approximately 11:06 p.m. on or about September 1, 2004, during the course of the Republican National Convention, Defendant BILL O'REILLY telephoned Plaintiff ANDREA MACKRIS on her cell phone and asked that she call. Plaintiff believed that the call

would be work-related, and returned the call. Instead, Defendant **BILL O'REILLY** once again launched into a lewd and lascivious, unsolicited and disturbing sexually-graphic talk.

➤ 77.   Despite informing him that she was not at all interested in the conversation, and despite her adamant refusal to participate in such talk, Defendant **O'REILLY** informed Plaintiff **ANDREA MACKRIS** that he was watching a porn movie and babbled perversely regarding his fantasies concerning Carribean vacations because, purportedly: "Once people get into that hot weather they shed their inhibitions, you know they drink during the day, they lay there and lazy, they have dinner and then they come back and fool around... that's basically the modus operandi."

78.   During the course of his monologue, Defendant **O'REILLY** further stated:

> Well, if I took you down there then I'd want to take a shower with you right away, that would be the first think I'd do... yeah, we'd check into the room, and we would order up some room service and uh and you'd definitely get two wines into you as quickly as I could get into you I would get 'em into you... maybe intravenously, get those glasses of wine into you....
>
> You would basically be in the shower and then I would come in and I'd join you and you would have your back to me and I would take that little loofa thing and kinda' soap up your back... rub it all over you, get you to relax, hot water... and um... you know, you'd feel the tension drain out of you and uh you still would be with your back to me then I would kinda' put my arm - it's one of those mitts, those loofa mitts you know, so I got my hands in it... and I would put it around front, kinda' rub your tummy a little bit with it, and then with my other hand I would start to massage your boobs, get your nipples really hard... 'cuz I like that and you have really spectacular boobs....
>
> So anyway I'd be rubbing your big boobs and getting your nipples really hard, kinda' kissing your neck from behind... and then I would take the other hand with the falafel (sic) thing and I'd put it on your pussy but you'd have to do it really light, just kind of a tease business....

Plaintiff **ANDREA MACKRIS** was frightened and disturbed.

79.   During the course of this monologue, Defendant **BILL O'REILLY** suggested that he would perform oral sex upon Plaintiff **ANDREA MACKRIS**, and that she would start to perform fellatio upon his "big cock" but not complete the sex act: "you'd tease me, like you wouldn't really do it, you'd just like - 'cuz I know you... you're like a tease."

80.   During the course of his perverted ravings, Defendant **BILL O'REILLY** told Plaintiff that they would then engage in sexual intercourse. When Plaintiff **ANDREA MACKRIS** again reminded Defendant **O'REILLY** that she did not want to participate reminding him that he was her boss, **O'REILLY** responded: "you just have to suspend that."

81.   During the course of Defendant **BILL O'REILLY**'s sexual rant, it became clear that he was using a vibrator upon himself, and that he ejaculated. Plaintiff was repulsed.

82.   Immediately after climaxing, Defendant **BILL O'REILLY** launched into a discussion concerning how good he was during a recent appearance on "The Tonight Show" with Jay Leno: "It was funny, they used a big clip of me.... Right after Brokaw and Brokaw was absolutely the most unfunny guy in the world, and the audience got a big charge out of my.... It was good."

83.   After climaxing, Defendant **BILL O'REILLY** again boasted that none of the women he'd engaged in sexual relations with would ever tell:

> Nobody'd believe 'em... they wouldn't [tell] anyway, I can't imagine any of them ever doing that 'cuz I always made friends with women before I bedded them down.

84.   Defendant **BILL O'REILLY** concluded stating:

> You know, Mackris, in these days of your celibacy and your hibernation this is good for you to have a little fantasy outlet,

you know, just to keep it tuned, keep that sensuality tuned until you know Mr. Right comes along and then you can put him in traction.... I'm trying to tell you, this is good for your mental health.

Plaintiff ANDREA MACKRIS felt angry, abused and disgusted.

85. On or about September 21, 2004, Defendant BILL O'REILLY telephoned Plaintiff ANDREA MACKRIS and, once again, without invitation or solicitation, launched into yet another disgusting, lewd and disturbing monologue concerning his sexual fantasies with her, until he climaxed. During the course of this call, O'REILLY said to Plaintiff: "Next time you'll come up to my hotel room and we'll make this happen." Plaintiff felt frightened and threatened.

AS AND FOR A FIRST CAUSE OF ACTION
NYSHRL - QUID PRO QUO SEXUAL HARASSMENT

86. Plaintiff ANDREA MACKRIS repeats and realleges each and every allegation contained in paragraphs 1 through 85 inclusive, with the same force and effect as though more fully set forth at length herein.

87. The aforesaid acts of intentional *quid pro quo* sexual harassment, perpetrated by Defendant BILL O'REILLY violated Plaintiff ANDREA MACKRIS' rights as provided under New York State Human Rights Law - Executive Law Section 290 et. seq.

88. As a consequence of Defendant BILL O'REILLY's sexual harassment during Plaintiff's employment at Defendants FOX and WESTWOOD ONE, Plaintiff sustained conscious pain and suffering, physical injury, great mental distress, shock, fright and humiliation.

89. As a consequence of the foregoing misconduct of Defendants, Plaintiff ANDREA MACKRIS has been damaged in an amount exceeding the jurisdictional requirements of this Court.

AS AND FOR A SECOND CAUSE OF ACTION
NYSHRL - SEXUAL HARASSMENT

90.   Plaintiff ANDREA MACKRIS repeats and realleges each and every allegation contained in paragraphs 1 through 85 inclusive, with the same force and effect as though more fully set forth at length herein.

91.   The aforesaid acts of intentional *quid pro quo* sexual harassment, perpetrated by Defendant BILL O'REILLY, an employee of Defendants FOX, their officers, directors, supervisors, managers and/or employees, violated Plaintiff ANDREA MACKRIS' rights as provided under New York State Human Rights Law - Executive Law Section 290 et. seq.

92.   As a consequence of Plaintiff's sexual harassment by her supervisor, Defendant BILL O'REILLY during Plaintiff's employment at Defendants FOX, Plaintiff sustained conscious pain and suffering, physical injury, great mental distress, shock, fright and humiliation.

93.   As a consequence of the foregoing misconduct of Defendants FOX, Plaintiff ANDREA MACKRIS has been damaged in an amount exceeding the jurisdictional requirements of this Court.

AS AND FOR A THIRD CAUSE OF ACTION
NYSHRL - SEXUAL HARASSMENT

94.   Plaintiff ANDREA MACKRIS repeats and realleges each and every allegation contained in paragraphs 1 through 85 inclusive, with the same force and effect as though more fully set forth at length herein.

95.   The aforesaid acts of intentional *quid pro quo* sexual harassment, perpetrated by Defendant BILL O'REILLY, an employee of Defendant WESTWOOD ONE, their officers, directors, supervisors, managers and/or employees, violated Plaintiff ANDREA MACKRIS' rights as provided under New York State Human Rights Law - Executive Law Section 290 et.

seq.

96.   As a consequence of Plaintiff's sexual harassment by her supervisor, Defendant BILL O'REILLY during Plaintiff's employment at Defendant WESTWOOD ONE, Plaintiff sustained conscious pain and suffering, physical injury, great mental distress, shock, fright and humiliation.

97.   As a consequence of the foregoing misconduct of Defendant WESTWOOD ONE, Plaintiff ANDREA MACKRIS has been damaged in an amount exceeding the jurisdictional requirements of this Court.

AS AND FOR A FOURTH CAUSE OF ACTION
NYSHRL - SEXUALLY HOSTILE WORK ENVIRONMENT

98.   Plaintiff ANDREA MACKRIS repeats and realleges each and every allegation contained in paragraphs 1 through 85 inclusive, with the same force and effect as though more fully set forth at length herein.

99.   The sexually hostile work environment created by the sexual harassment of Defendant BILL O'REILLY during Plaintiff's employment at Defendants FOX, and perpetuated by Defendants FOX, its officers, directors, supervisors, managers and/or employees violated Plaintiff ANDREA MACKRIS' rights as provided under New York State Human Rights Law - Executive Law Section 290 et. seq.

100.   As a consequence of the sexually hostile work environment created by Defendants FOX, Plaintiff sustained conscious pain and suffering, physical injury, great mental distress, shock, fright and humiliation, and incurred monetary loss.

101.   As a consequence of the foregoing misconduct of Defendants, Plaintiff ANDREA MACKRIS has been damaged in an amount exceeding the jurisdictional requirements of this

Court.

AS AND FOR A FIFTH CAUSE OF ACTION
NYSHRL - SEXUALLY HOSTILE WORK ENVIRONMENT

102.   Plaintiff ANDREA MACKRIS repeats and realleges each and every allegation

contained in paragraphs 1 through 85 inclusive, with the same force and effect as though more

fully set forth at length herein.

103.   The sexually hostile work environment created by the sexual harassment of

Defendant BILL O'REILLY during Plaintiff's employment at Defendant WESTWOOD ONE,

and perpetuated by Defendant WESTWOOD ONE, its officers, directors, supervisors, managers

and/or employees violated Plaintiff ANDREA MACKRIS' rights as provided under New York

State Human Rights Law - Executive Law Section 290 et. seq.

104.   As a consequence of the sexually hostile work environment created by Defendant

WESTWOOD ONE, Plaintiff sustained conscious pain and suffering, physical injury, great

mental distress, shock, fright and humiliation.

105.   As a consequence of the foregoing misconduct of Defendants, Plaintiff ANDREA

MACKRIS has been damaged in an amount exceeding the jurisdictional requirements of this

Court.

WHEREFORE, Plaintiff ANDREA MACKRIS demands judgment against Defendant

BILL O'REILLY in the First Cause of Action in an amount exceeding the jurisdictional

requirements of this Court;   Plaintiff ANDREA MACKRIS demands judgment against

Defendants FOX in the Second Cause of Action in an amount exceeding the jurisdictional

requirements of this Court;   Plaintiff ANDREA MACKRIS demands judgment against

Defendants WESTWOOD ONE in the Third Cause of Action in an amount exceeding the jurisdictional requirements of this Court; Plaintiff ANDREA MACKRIS demands judgment against Defendants FOX in the Fourth Cause of Action in an amount exceeding the jurisdictional requirements of this Court; and Plaintiff ANDREA MACKRIS demands judgment against Defendants WESTWOOD ONE in the Fifth Cause of Action in an amount exceeding the jurisdictional requirements of this Court, all together with the costs and disbursements of this action, including attorneys' fees, plus interest, and for any other relief which this Court deems just and proper.

Dated: New York, New York
          September 28, 2004

BENEDICT P. MORELLI & ASSOCIATES, P.C

By: _____

Benedict P. Morelli, Esq.
David S. Ratner, Esq.
Martha M. McBrayer, Esq.
950 Third Avenue, 11th Floor
New York, New York 10022
(212) 751-9800

APPENDIX B-1

Entered By: Jacalyn Hudlemeyer, On 6/12/2007 12:42:46 PM
Edited By: Dave Karsnia, On 6/26/2007 8:58:07 AM

Title: Lewd Conduct

07002008

On 06/11/07, at about 1200 hours, I was working a plain-clothes detail involving lewd conduct in the main man's public restroom of the Northstar Crossing in the Lindbergh Terminal. The Airport Police Department has received civilian complaints and has made numerous arrests regarding sexual activity in the public restroom.

I entered the men's restroom and proceeded to an unoccupied stall in the back of the restroom. Other people were in the restroom for their intended purposes. Some, but not all of the bathroom stalls were occupied. While seated in the stall, I was the third stall from the wall which was to my left (East). From my seated position, I could observe the shoes and ankles of person seated to the right of me. An unidentified person entered the stall to the left of me. From my seated position, I was able to see his shoes and ankles.

At 1213 hours, I could see an older white male with grey hair standing outside my stall. He was standing about three feet away and had a roller bag with him. The male was later identified by ██████ driver's license as Larry Edwin Craig ██████. I could see Craig look through the crack in the door from his position. Craig would look down at his hands, 'fidget' with his fingers, and then look through the crack into my stall again. Craig would repeat this cycle for about two minutes. I was able to see Craig's blue eyes as he looked into my stall.

At 1215 hours, the male in the stall to the left of me flushed the toilet and exited the stall. Craig entered the stall and placed his roller bag against the front of the stall door. My experience has shown that individuals engaging in lewd conduct use their bags to block the view from the front of their stall. From my seated position, I could observe the shoes and ankles of Craig seated to the left of me. He was wearing dress pants with black dress shoes. At 1216 hours, Craig tapped his right foot. I recognized this as a signal used by persons wishing to engage in lewd conduct. Craig tapped his toes several times and moved his foot closer to my foot. I moved my foot up and down slowly. While this was occurring, the male in the stall to my right was still present. I could hear several unknown persons in the restroom that appeared to use the restroom for its intended use. The presence of others did not seem to deter Craig as he moved his right foot so that it touched the side of my left foot which was within my stall area.

At 1217 hours, I saw Craig swipe his hand under the stall divider for a few seconds. The swipe went in the direction from the front (door side) of the stall back towards the back wall. His palm was facing towards the ceiling as he guided it all the stall divider. I was only able to see the tips of his fingers on my side of the stall divider. Craig swiped his hand again for a few seconds in the same motion to where I could see more of his fingers. Craig then swiped his hand in the same motion a third time for a few seconds. I could see that it was Craig's left hand due to the position of his thumb. I could also see Craig had a gold ring on his ring finger as his hand was on my side of the stall divider.

At about 1219 hours, I held my Police identification in my right hand down by the floor so that Craig could see it. With my left hand near the floor, I pointed towards the exit. Craig responded, "No!" I again pointed towards the exit. Craig exited the stall with his roller bags without flushing the toilet. Without causing a disturbance, I discretely motioned for Craig to exit the restroom. I noticed that

██████████████████████████████████████

not all of the stalls were occupied. Craig demanded to see my credentials. I again showed Craig my credentials. Craig kept asking what was going to happen. I told Craig that we would speak in private. Craig said that he would not go. I told Craig that he was under arrest, he had to go, and that I didn't want to make a scene. Craig then left the restroom.

Once outside the restroom, Craig stopped near the entrance and was hesitant to comply. I told Craig that we would speak in a private area without embarrassing him or causing a disturbance. Craig was still hesitant to follow me at first, but then complied. He followed me towards the Police Operations Center (POC). Detective Nelson was seated outside of the restroom and followed us. Dispatch was notified that we had one in custody at 1222 hours.

When we got to the POC, we asked Craig to leave his bags outside of the interview room. This is standard procedure for safety reasons. I asked him for his driver's license. Craig left his roller bag outside the interview room, but brought his two-strapped carry bag in with him. I again stated that he had to leave the bag outside. Craig stated that his identification was in the bag. Craig handed me a business card that identified himself as a United States Senator as he stated, "What do you think about that?" I responded by setting his business card down on the table and again asking him for his driver's license.

Craig provided me his Idaho driver's license. In a recorded post-Miranda interview, Craig stated the following:
- He is a commuter
- He went into the bathroom
- He was standing outside of the stalls for 1-2 minutes waiting for the stall.
- He has a wide stance when going to the bathroom and that his foot may have touched mine
- He reached down with his right hand to pick up a piece of paper that was on the floor
- He is unable to take his gold wedding ring off of his left ring finger

It should be noted that there was not a piece of paper on the bathroom floor, nor did Craig pick up a piece of paper. During the interview, Craig either disagreed with me or "didn't recall" the events as they happened.

Craig was worried about missing his flight. Detective Nelson tried to call the airline to hold the plane. The airline did not answer the phone. Craig's Criminal History was clear. Craig was explained the process for formal complaints. Craig was photographed, fingerprinted, and released pending formal complaint for Interference with Privacy (MSS 609.746) and Disorderly Conduct (609.72) at 1305 hours.

Sgt. Karsnia #4211
Airport Police Department

APPENDIX B-2

FILED

AUG 8 2007

HENNEPIN COUNTY DISTRICT
COURT DEPUTY

STATE OF MINNESOTA   DISTRICT COURT

COUNTY OF HENNEPIN   FOURTH JUDICIAL DISTRICT

Case No. <u>07043231</u>

State of Minnesota,

                    Plaintiff,   **PETITION TO ENTER**

    vs   **PLEA OF GUILTY-MISDEMEANOR**

Larry Edwin Craig,

                    Defendant.

I, Larry Edwin Craig, am the defendant in the above action. My date of birth is July 20, 1945. I state to the court that:

1.   I have reviewed the arrest report and/or complaint relating to the charges against me.

2.   I understand the charge(s) made against me in this case, which are: Disorderly Conduct, pursuant to Minn. Stat. § 609.72 subd. 1(3), a Misdemeanor; and Interference with Privacy, pursuant to Minn. Stat. § 609.746, subd. 1(c), a Gross Misdemeanor. I am pleading guilty to the offense of Disorderly Conduct as a Misdemeanor.

3.   I am pleading guilty to the charge of Disorderly Conduct as alleged because on June 11, 2007, within the property or jurisdiction of the Metropolitan Airports Commission, Hennepin County, specifically in the restroom of the North Star Crossing in the Lindbergh Terminal, I did the following: Engaged in conduct which I knew or should have known tended to arouse alarm or resentment or others which conduct was physical (versus verbal) in nature.

4.   I understand that the court will not accept a plea of guilty from anyone who claims to be innocent.

5.   I now make no claim that I am innocent of the charge to which I am entering a plea of guilty.

Larry Edwin Craig, Defendant

1

APPENDIX B-3

Investigative Sgt. Dave Karsnia #4211 and Detective Noel Nelson of the Minneapolis Police Department intert 1162

(NN) INTERVIEW WITH Larry Craig (LC) Case 07002008

Larry Craig: Am I gonna have to fight you in court?

Dave Karsnia: No. No. I'm not gonna go to court unless you want me there.

LC: Cause I don't want to be in court either.

DK: Ok. I don't either.

(inaudible) **DK:** Urn, here's the way it works, urn, you'll you'll be released today, okay.

LC: Okay.

DK: All right. I, I know I can bring you to jail, but that's not my goal here, okay? (inaudible)

LC: Don't do that. You You

DK: I'm not going to bring you to jail

LC: You solicited me.

DK: Okay. We're going to get, We're going to get into that. (inaudible)

LC: Okay.

DK: But there's the, there there's two ways, yes. You can, you can, ah, you can go to court. You can plead guilty.

LC: Yep.

DK: There'll be a fine. You won't have to explain anything. (inaudible) I know.

LC: Right.

DK: And you'll pay a fine, you be (inaudible), done. Or if you want to plead not guilty, ah, and I, I can't make these decisions for you.

LC: No, no. Just tell me where I am (inaudible) I need to make this flight.

DK: Okay. Okay. And then I go to people that are not guilty, then I would have to come to court and end up testifying. So those are the two things, okay. Did I explain that part?

LC: Yes

DK: Okay Urn, ah, I'm just going to read you your rights real quick, okay? You got it on?

Noel Nelson: Yep.

DK: Okay.

DK: Ah, the date is 6/11/07 at 1228 hours. Urn, Mr. Craig?

LC: Yes.

DK. Sorry about that. (ringing phone)

DK: You have the right to remain silent. Anything you say can and will be used against you in court of law. You have the right to talk to a lawyer now or have a present, a lawyer present now or anytime during questioning. If you cannot afford a lawyer, one will be appointed to you without cost. Do you understand each of these rights the way I have explained them to you?

LC: I do.

DK: Do you wish to talk to us at this time?

LC: I do

DK: Okay Urn, I just wanna start off with a your side of the story, okay. So, a

LC: So I go into the bathroom here as I normally do, I'm a commuter too here.

DK: Okay.

LC: I sit down, urn, to go to the bathroom and ah, you said our feet bumped. I believe they did, ah, because I reached down and scooted over and urn, the next thing I knew, under the bathroom divider comes a card that says Police. Now, urn, (sigh) that's about as far as I can take it, I don't know of anything else. Ah, your foot came toward mine, mine came towards yours, was that natural? I don't know. Did we bump? Yes. I think we did. You said so. I don't disagree with that.

DK: Okay. I don't want to get into a pissing match here.

LC: We're not going to.

DK: Good. Urn,

LC: I don't, ah, I am not gay, I don't do these kinds of things and...

DK: It doesn't matter, I don't care about sexual preference or anything like that. Here's your stuff back sir. Urn, I don't care about sexual preference.

LC: I know you don't. You're out to enforce the law.

DK: Right.

LC: But you shouldn't be out to entrap people either.

DK: This isn't entrapment.

LC: All right.

DK: Urn, you you're skipping some parts here, but what what about your hand?

LC: What about it? I reached down, my foot like this. There was a piece of paper on the floor, I picked it up

DK: Okay.

LC: What about my hand?

DK: Well, you're not being truthful with me, I'm kinda disappointed in you Senator. I'm real disappointed in you right now. Okay. I'm not, just so you know, just like everybody, 1,1,1, treat with dignity, I try to pull them away from the situation

LC: 1,1

DK: and not embarrass them.

LC: I appreciate that.

DK: And I

LC: You did that after the stall.

DK: I will say every person I've had so far has told me the truth. We've been respectful to each other and then they've gone on their way. And I've never had to bring anybody to jail because everybody's been truthful to me.

LC: I don't want you to take me to jail and I think.

DK: I'm not gonna take you to jail as long as your cooperative but I'm not gonna lie. We...

LC: Did my hand come below the divider? Yes. It did.

DK: Okay, sir. We deal with people that lie to us every day.

LC: I'm sure you do.

DK: I'm sure you do to sir.

LC: And gentleman so do I.

DK: I'm sure you do. We deal with a lot of people that are very bad people. You're not a bad person.

LC: No, I don't think I am.

DK: Okay, so what I'm telling you, I don't want to be lied to.

LC: Okay.

DK: Okay. So we'll start over, you're gonna get out of here. You're gonna have to pay a fine and that will be it. Okay. I don't call media, I don't do any of that type of crap.

LC: Fine.

DK: Okay.

LC: Fine.

DK: All right, so let's start from the beginning. You went in the bathroom.

LC: I went in the bathroom.

DK: And what did you do when you...

LC: 1 stood beside the wall, waiting for a stall to open. I got in the stall, sat down, and I started to go to the bathroom. Ah, did our feet come together, apparently they did bump. Well, I won't dispute that.

DK: Okay. When I got out of the stall, I noticed other other stalls were open.

LC: They were at the time. At the time I entered, 1,1, at the time I entered, I stood and waited.

DK: Okay.

LC: They were all busy, you know?

DK: Were you (inaudible) out here while you were waiting? I could see your eyes. I saw you playing with your fingers and then look up. Play with your fingers and then look up.

LC: Did I glance at your stall? I was glancing at a stall right beside yours waiting for a fella to empty it. I saw him stand up and therefore I thought it was going to empty.

DK: How long do you think you stood outside the stalls?

LC: Oh a minute or two at the most.

DK: Okay. And when you went in the stalls, then what?

LC: Sat down.

DK: Okay. Did you do anything with your feet?

LC: Positioned them, I don't know. I don't know at the time. I'm a fairly wide guy.

DK: I understand.

LC: I had to spread my legs.

DK: Okay.

LC: When I lower my pants so they won't slide.

DK: Okay.

LC: Did I slide them too close to yours? Did I, I looked down once, your foot was close to mine.

DK: Yes.

LC: Did we bump? Ah, you said so, I don't recall that, but apparently we were close.

DK: Yeah, well your foot did touch mine, on my side of the stall.

LC: All right.

DK: Okay. And then with the hand. Urn, how many times did you put your hand under the stall?

LC: I don't recall. I remember reaching down once. There was a piece of toilet paper back behind me and picking it up.

DK: Okay. Was your was your palm down or up when you were doing that?

LC: I don't recall.

DK: Okay. I recall your palm being up. Okay.

LC: All right.

DK: When you pick up a piece of paper off the ground, your palm would be down, when you pick something up.

LC: Yeah, probably would be. I recall picking the paper up.

DK: And I know it's hard to describe here on tape but actually what I saw was your fingers come underneath the stalls, you're actually ta touching the bottom of the stall divider.

LC: I don't recall that.

DK: You don't recall

LC: I don't believe I did that. I don't.

DK: I saw, I saw

LC: I don't do those things.

DK: I saw your left hand and I could see the gold wedding ring when it when it went across. I could see that. On your left hand, I could see that. LC: Wait a moment, my left hand was over here.

DK: I saw there's a...

LC: My right hand was next to you.

DK: I could tell it with my ah, I could tell it was your left hand because your thumb was positioned in a faceward motion. Your thumb was on this side, not on this side.

LC: Well, we can dispute that. I'm not going to fight you in court and I, I reached down with my right hand to pick up the paper.

DK: But I'm telling you that I could see that so I know that's your left hand. Also I could see a gold ring on this finger, so that's obvious it was the left hand.

LC: Yeah, okay. My left hand was in the direct opposite of the stall from you.

DK: Okay. You, you travel through here frequently correct?

LC: I do

DK: Um,

LC: Almost weekly.

DK: Have you been successful in these bathrooms here before?

LC: I go to that bathroom regularly

DK: I mean for any type of other activities.

LC: No. Absolutely not. I don't seek activity in bathrooms.

DK: It's embarrassing.

LC: Well it's embarrassing for both.. I'm not gonna fight you.

DK: I know you're not going to fight me. But that's not the point. I would respect you and I still respect you. I don't disrespect you but I'm disrespected right now and I'm not trying to act like I have all kinds of power or anything, but you're sitting here lying to a police officer.

DK: It's not a (inaudible) I'm getting from somebody else. I'm (inaudible)

LC: (inaudible) (Talking over each other)

DK: I am trained in this and I know what I am doing. And I say you put your hand under there and you're going to sit there and...

LC: I admit I put my hand down.

DK: You put your hand and rubbed it on the bottom of the stall with your left hand.

LC: No. Wait a moment.

DK: And I, I'm not dumb, you can say I don't recall...

LC: If I had turned sideways, that was the only way I could get my left hand over there.

DK: it's not that hard for me to reach. (inaudible) it's not that hard. I see it happen every day out here now.

LC: (inaudible) you do. All right.

DK: I just, I just, I guess, I guess I'm gonna say I'm just disappointed in you sir. I'm just really am. I expect this from the guy that we get out of the hood. I mean, people vote for you.

LC: Yes, they do. (inaudible)

DK: unbelievable, unbelievable.

LC: I'm a respectable person and I don't do these kinds of...

DK: And (inaudible) respect right now though

LC: But I didn't use my left hand.

DK: I thought that you...

LC: I reached down with my right hand like this to pick up a piece of paper.

DK: Was your gold ring on your right hand at anytime today.

LC: Of course not, try to get it off, look at it.

DK: Okay. Then it was your left hand, I saw it with my own eyes.

LC: All right, you saw something that didn't happen.

DK: Embarrassing, embarrassing. No wonder why we're going down the tubes. Anything to add?

NN: Uh, no

DK: Embarrassing. Date is 6/11/07 at 1236 interview is done.

LC: Okay

APPENDIX C

AGENCY NAME	( ) OFCR SAFETY ( ) OFCR ASSAULT	RESP	ASGN	PROPERTY ☐ YES ☐ NO	INCIDENT NUMBER 07-808376

SPD

<table>
<tr><td rowspan="2">TYPE OF REPORT</td><td>(✓) PERSONS
( ) PROPERTY
( ) INFORMATION</td><td>( ) VEHICLE
( ) ARREST
( ) PHONE REPORT</td><td>( ) JUVENILE
( ) CHILD ABUSE
( ) DOMESTIC VIOLENCE</td><td>( ) HATE/BIAS
( ) ARSON-LOSS $
( ) OTHER:</td><td>( ) COMPUTER USED
( ) DRUG RELATED
( ) ALCOHOL RELATED</td></tr>
</table>

DATA

INCIDENT CLASSIFICATION		OFFENSE CODES						
EXTORTION			A	C	A	C	A C	A C

ADDRESS/LOCATION OF INCIDENT	PREMISE TYPE/NAME	# OF UNITS ENTERED	CODE	GEO CODES
S 111 POST RM 968				2

REPORTED ON					OCCURRED ON OR FROM					OCCURRED TO				
MONTH	DAY	YEAR	TIME	DOW	MONTH	DAY	YEAR	TIME	DOW	MONTH	DAY	YEAR	TIME	DOW
10	26	07	1131		10	26	07	0700					1330	

ADD'L ON	( ) PERSONS ( ) VEHICLES ( ) COLLISION RPT.	CODES:	V - VICTIM W - WITNESS O - OTHERS	B - VICT. BUSINESS C - COMPLAINANT G - PARENT/GUARDIAN	D - DECEASED RO - REG. OWNER	LANDLORD NOTIFICATION Y N NAME

PERSONS / BUSINESSES

NO.	NON-DISC.	NAME (LAST, FIRST, MIDDLE)	AFFILIATION	RACE	ETH	SEX	D.O.B./AGE	HGT	WGT	HAIR	EYES
C		CURTISS, RICHARD LYNN		W₃	3		57				

STREET ADDRESS	APT.#	CITY		STATE	ZIP	RES STATUS: F P NO U

RESIDENCE PHONE	BUSINESS PHONE	EMPLOYMENT/OCCUPATION/SCHOOL	HATE/BIAS CODE	TYPE VICTIM	TYPE INJURY	VICTIM OF OFNS.# OFNDR.#	RELATIONSHIP CODE

NO.	NON-	NAME (LAST, FIRST, MIDDLE)	AFFILIATION	RACE	ETH	SEX	D.O.B./AGE	HGT	WGT	HAIR	EYES
W₁		HENNEMAN, JALENE M.					76				

STREET ADDRESS	APT.#	CITY		STATE	ZIP	RES STATUS: F P NO U

RESIDENCE PHONE	BUSINESS PHONE	EMPLOYMENT/OCCUPATION/SCHOOL	HATE/BIAS CODE	TYPE VICTIM	TYPE INJURY	VICTIM OF OFNS.# OFNDR.#	RELATIONSHIP CODE

NUMBER OF SUSPECTS/ARRESTED PERSONS IN THIS INCIDENT:	SUSPECT CODES:	A - ARREST R - RUNAWAY	S - SUSPECT M - MISSING	I - INSTITUTIONAL (MENTAL/DETOX)	X - OTHER

VEHICLE / TRLR / BOAT

VEHICLE CODES:	( ) STOLEN # ( ) RECOVERED #	( ) LOCATED ( ) TOWED ( ) EVIDENCE	( ) SEIZED ( ) ABANDONING	( ) DAMAGED/VANDALIZED ( ) OTHER	( ) VICTIMS VEH. ( ) SUSPECTS VEH.	( ) HOLD - FOR:

NO.	LICENSE NUMBER	STATE	VIN/HULL NO.	YEAR	MAKE	MODEL	STYLE
S							

COLOR	SPECIAL FEATURES/DESCRIPTION	VALUE$	DRIVER IS: ( ) R/O ( ) PERSON #	REGISTERED OWNERS NAME
	R/O -			

		TOW COMPANY/ADDRESS/PHONE	STATE TOW NO.	REGISTERED OWNERS ADDRESS

VEHICLE DISPOSITION ( ) LEFT AT SCENE ( ) DRIVEN AWAY ( ) TOWED							SPECIFY DAMAGE BY SHADING DAMAGED AREA	DAMAGE EST. $
LOCKED Y N	KEYS IN VEHICLE Y N	DELINQ. PAYMENT Y N	VICTIM CONSENT Y N	THEFT INS. Y N	DRIVE-ABLE Y N	DAMAGE TO VEHICLE Y N	7 5 3 1 / 8 6 4 2	

SIGNATURE

FALSE REPORTING: A PERSON COMMITS THE CRIME OF **MAKING A FALSE REPORT** IF HE/SHE WILLFULLY MAKES ANY UNTRUE, MISLEADING OR EXAGGERATED STATEMENT TO EITHER THE POLICE OR FIRE DEPARTMENT. MAKING SUCH A FALSE REPORT IS A MISDEMEANOR. BY SIGNING BELOW, YOU ARE CERTIFYING THAT:
- YOU DID NOT GIVE PERMISSION FOR ANYONE TO ENTER YOUR PREMISES AND/OR TO TAKE/REMOVE YOUR PROPERTY/VEHICLE.
- YOU UNDERSTAND THAT IF LAW ENFORCEMENT OFFICERS LOCATE THIS VEHICLE AND YOU CANNOT BE CONTACTED OR YOU ARE UNABLE TO RESPOND TO THE SCENE OF THE RECOVERY WITHIN 30 MINUTES, THE VEHICLE WILL BE TOWED TO A PLACE OF SAFEKEEPING AT YOUR EXPENSE.
- IF THIS IS A FOUND PROPERTY REPORT, YOU HAVE BEEN ADVISED OF CHAPTER 63 OF THE R.C.W AND THAT YOU ( ) DO ( ) DO NOT WANT TO CLAIM THE PROPERTY IF THE TRUE OWNER CANNOT BE FOUND. PREFERRED TOW COMPANY _____
- YOU HAVE READ AND UNDERSTAND THE ABOVE.

SIGNATURE OF PERSON MAKING THIS REPORT	DATE

STATUS

( ) Officer/Deputy released property to _____	( ) The named juvenile is currently a runway	( ) The named person is currently missing

OFFICER NAME/NUMBER 366	AREA	OFFICER NAME/NUMBER	AREA	APPROVED BY	BOOKING APPROVED BY	ASSIGNED
J. H. MADSEN						

IBR CLEARANCE ( ) ARR/A ( ) EXC/A ( ) ARR/J ( ) EXC/J	ADMIN CLEARANCE ( ) WARRANT ( ) SUSPENDED	DISTRIBUTION ( ) CA ( ) PA	( ) CPS ( ) DSHS	( ) JUV ( ) MH	( ) HD ( ) DET ( ) PAT	OTHER:	DATA ENTRY

PROPERTY / NARRATIVE REPORT

Rev. 2/06

Page _____ Of _____

| TYPE OF ACTION: | 1 - STOLEN 2 - LOST 3 - DESTROYED/DAMAGED/VANDALIZED | 4 - COUNTERFEIT/FORGED 5 - BURNED 6 - INVESTIGATIVE INFO. | 7- UNKNOWN _____ 8 - NONE _____ 9 - RECOVERED BY VICTIM | INCIDENT NUMBER |

PROPERTY DESCRIPTION for DESC CODE blocks

01	AIRCRAFT	15	HEAVY CONSTRUCTION/INDUSTRIAL EQUIPMENT	29	STRUCTURES - SINGLE DWELLINGS
02	ALCOHOL	16	JEWELRY/PRECIOUS METALS	30	STRUCTURES - OTHER DWELLINGS
03	AUTOMOBILE	17	HOUSEHOLD GOODS	31	STRUCTURES - OTHER COMMERCIAL /BUSINESS
04	BICYCLES	18	LIVESTOCK	32	STRUCTURES - INDUST./MFG.
05	BUSES	19	MERCHANDISE	33	STRUCTURES - PUBLIC/COMMUNITY
06	CLOTHING/FURS	20	MONEY	34	STRUCTURES - STORAGE
07	COMPUTER HARDWARE/SOFTWARE	21	NEGOTIABLE INSTRUMENTS	35	STRUCTURES - OTHER
08	CONSUMABLE GOODS	22	NON-NEGOTIABLE INSTRUMENTS	36	TOOLS - POWER/HAND
09	CREDIT/DEBIT CARDS	23	OFFICE - TYPE EQUIPMENT	37	TRUCKS
10	DRUGS/NARCOTICS	24	OTHER MOTOR VEHICLES	38	VEHICLE PARTS/ACCESSORIES
11	DRUGS/NARCOTICS EQUIPMENT/PARAPH.	25	PURSES/HANDBAGS/WALLETS	39	WATERCRAFT
12	FARM EQUIPMENT	26	RADIOS/TELEVISIONS/VISUAL	88	PENDING INVENTORY
13	FIREARMS	27	RECORDINGS - AUDIO/VISUAL	98	RESERVED FOR SPECIAL USE
14	GAMBLING EQUIPMENT	28	RECREATIONAL VEHICLES	99	OTHER (INCLUDES INTANGIBLES)

No.	ITEM		SERIAL/OAN	BRAND NAME	MODEL/CALIBER
Action #	DESC. CODE	DESCRIPTION (IF WEAPON, INDICATE BARREL LENGTH, ACTION, FINISH)		MISC.	VALUE $
No.	ITEM		SERIAL/OAN	BRAND NAME	MODEL/CALIBER
Action #	DESC. CODE	DESCRIPTION (IF WEAPON, INDICATE BARREL LENGTH, ACTION, FINISH)		MISC.	VALUE $
No.	ITEM		SERIAL/OAN	BRAND NAME	MODEL/CALIBER
Action #	DESC. CODE	DESCRIPTION (IF WEAPON, INDICATE BARREL LENGTH, ACTION, FINISH)		MISC.	VALUE $
No.	ITEM		SERIAL/OAN	BRAND NAME	MODEL/CALIBER
Action #	DESC. CODE	DESCRIPTION (IF WEAPON, INDICATE BARREL LENGTH, ACTION, FINISH)		MISC.	VALUE $
No.	ITEM		SERIAL/OAN	BRAND NAME	MODEL/CALIBER
Action #	DESC. CODE	DESCRIPTION (IF WEAPON, INDICATE BARREL LENGTH, ACTION, FINISH)		MISC.	VALUE $

_____ SEE ADDITIONALS _____

_____ T H MADSEN #366 _____

| ENTERED: (INITIAL) | LOCAL | NCIC | WACIC | DATE | LETTER SENT Y   N |

1

SPOKANE POLICE DEPARTMENT
ADDITIONAL REPORT

<u>DATE/TIME:</u> 10/27/07   <u>CASE NO.:</u>   07-808376

<u>CHARGE/INCIDENT:</u>   EXTORTION

<u>FURTHER INVESTIGATION</u>   SGT. JOE PETERSON 076

On 10/27/07 at 0815 hours I was contacted by Lt. McGovern who requested that I respond to the Public Safety Building for a briefing reference an extortion.

At 0900 hours I was briefed by Lt. McGovern and Major Roberts.

At 1000 hours I contacted Det. Burbridge and requested that he assist in this case. Det. Madsen had been assigned this case on 10/26/07 and was also present.

At 1215 hours Det. Madsen and I contacted ███████████████ at ████ ██████████ Also present at that address was ██████ ██████ Deena Castagna. Det. Madsen had previously interviewed ████ and at this time told ████ that he had follow up questions to that interview. Both Deena Castagna and I were present when Det. Madsen told ████ that he was not under arrest, not in custody and no matter what happened would not be arrested on this date. Det. Madsen did say we were investigating a crime which would be forwarded to the Prosecutors Office. ████ agreed to speak with us. The interview was conducted on the outdoor back deck of the residence. Although Deena Castagna came out onto the deck several times to speak with ████ and to ask him if he was sure he wanted to continue the interview, she was not present for the majority of the questioning.

Det. Madsen offered ████ the option of having his interview recorded either by video or by audio tape recording and Cody declined, saying he was more comfortable talking us without being recorded.

The interview was concluded at 1412 hours. Det. Madsen had asked ████ for ██████ telephone during the interview. Det. Madsen told ████ that we were seizing the telephone as evidence and requested search consent from ████ to obtain the information in the telephone. ████ agreed and signed a search waiver consent card.

Det. Madsen and I left that residence at 1416 hours.

At 1525 hours Det. Madsen and I attempted to make contact at ███████████ which is the residence of Joey Castagna. No one answered the door and a card was left requesting that Det. Madsen be called.

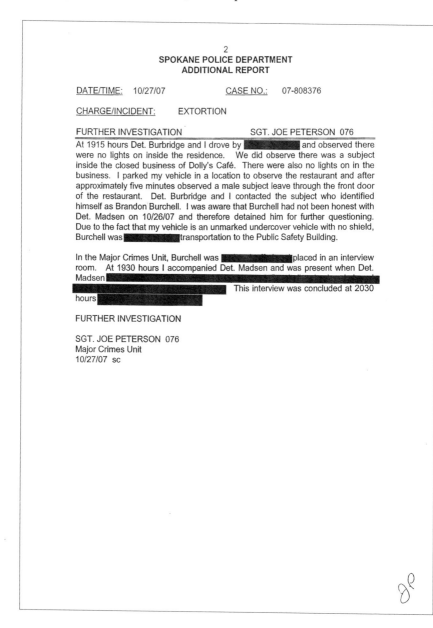

2
SPOKANE POLICE DEPARTMENT
ADDITIONAL REPORT

DATE/TIME: 10/27/07   CASE NO.:   07-808376

CHARGE/INCIDENT: EXTORTION

FURTHER INVESTIGATION   SGT. JOE PETERSON 076

At 1915 hours Det. Burbridge and I drove by ███████████ and observed there were no lights on inside the residence.   We did observe there was a subject inside the closed business of Dolly's Café.   There were also no lights on in the business.   I parked my vehicle in a location to observe the restaurant and after approximately five minutes observed a male subject leave through the front door of the restaurant.   Det. Burbridge and I contacted the subject who identified himself as Brandon Burchell.   I was aware that Burchell had not been honest with Det. Madsen on 10/26/07 and therefore detained him for further questioning. Due to the fact that my vehicle is an unmarked undercover vehicle with no shield, Burchell was ██████████████transportation to the Public Safety Building.

In the Major Crimes Unit, Burchell was ██████████████placed in an interview room.   At 1930 hours I accompanied Det. Madsen and was present when Det. Madsen ██ ████████████████████████████ This interview was concluded at 2030 hours ██████████████████████

FURTHER INVESTIGATION

SGT. JOE PETERSON 076
Major Crimes Unit
10/27/07 sc

1

SPOKANE POLICE DEPARTMENT
ADDITIONAL REPORT

DATE/TIME: 10/28/07   CASE NO.:   07-808376

CHARGE/INCIDENT: EXTORTION

FURTHER INVESTIGATION   DET. TIM MADSEN 366

On 10/28/07 at approximately 1100 hours I telephoned Richard Curtis. Curtis asked me what ▉▉▉▉ said had happened. I told Curtis ▉▉▉▉ claimed that Curtis said he would give ▉▉▉▉ $1,000 for allowing Curtis to perform "bareback" sex on the suspect. ▉▉▉▉ also said Curtis gave ▉▉▉▉ his billfold as collateral until Curtis paid the $1,000.

It should be noted that Curtis had previously denied offering ▉▉▉▉ any money for sex. He also previously denied having unprotected anal sex (bareback) with ▉▉▉▉ when I had interviewed Curtis on 10/27/07 over the phone.

Curtis told me that he believed he had been slipped some type of drug because he does not have a clear recollection of the activities that evening. Curtis first said he thought ▉▉▉▉ was lying about Curtis giving ▉▉▉▉ his billfold and the bareback sex. Curtis then stated he was so out of it he really didn't know what happened.

I asked Curtis why he had been in Spokane on 10/26/07. Curtis stated he was here on business. I asked Curtis what kind of business and Curtis said he had talked to his attorney who had advised Curtis not to talk to me any further. Curtis stated he did not want to be impolite but thought I had better talk to his attorney. Curtis said he did not understand why anything further was being done on this case and he felt like he was being treated as the suspect.

I asked Curtis who his attorney was and he stated he could not find the business card and he could not recall his attorney's name. I told Curtis once he found his attorney's name and information he could leave it on my voice mail.

On 10/28/07 I was reviewing the phone log on ▉▉▉▉ cell phone. I only saw one entry showing a phone number with a 360 area code. The phone number was ▉▉▉▉ The call was an incoming call dated 10/24/07. This would be the same area code as Richard Curtis' cell phone. The phone number was different than any number Curtis had given me. I called the phone number, ▉▉▉▉ It was a cell phone belonging to Steven Easterly, ▉▉83. Easterly stated he did not know ▉▉▉▉ He also said he did not know Richard Curtis. He thought maybe a friend of his had borrowed his cell phone to call ▉▉▉▉

Appendix C: Richard Curtis, Police Report

2

SPOKANE POLICE DEPARTMENT
ADDITIONAL REPORT

DATE/TIME: 10/28/07   CASE NO.:   07-808376

CHARGE/INCIDENT: EXTORTION

FURTHER INVESTIGATION   DET. TIM MADSEN   366

Steven Easterly told me that he resided at ▮▮▮▮▮▮▮▮ in Spokane, WA. The reason his cell phone had a 360 area code was because he had moved to Spokane from the Vancouver, WA area.   Easterly had no knowledge of this incident.

On 10/28/07 I talked to Leslie "Jo" McBride at the Holiday Gas Station in the 9700 block of N. Division. She gave me a video cassette from the surveillance cameras for 10/26/07. I had her check the time clock and she advised that the date was correct but the clock was running approximately four minutes faster than my watch, which showed the correct current time. I placed the video cassette into property as evidence.

FURTHER INVESTIGATION

DETECTIVE TIM MADSEN 366
Major Crimes Unit
10/28/07 sc

1

SPOKANE POLICE DEPARTMENT
ADDITIONAL REPORT

DATE/TIME: 10/27/07   CASE NO.: 07-808376

CHARGE/INCIDENT: EXTORTION

FURTHER INVESTIGATION   DET. TIM MADSEN 366

COMP: RICHARD LYN CURTIS, WM, ██ 59, ███████████
██

           BRANDON DEAN BURCHELL, WM, ███/83, ███████
█████████████████████████████

MIR: JOSEPH LEON CASTAGNA, WM, ██████ 82, ███████
████████████████████

On 10/26/07 Lt. Dave McGovern requested that I investigate a possible extortion involving reported victim Richard Lyn Curtis. Curtis was reportedly a member of the Washington State House of Representatives. Curtis had sexual relations with a male while staying at the Davenport Towers, located at 111 S. Post. The male suspect reportedly stole Curtis' billfold and was threatening to report their homosexual activities unless he was paid $1,000.

Lt. McGovern and I met Richard Curtis and Sgt. Ken Wade of the Washington State Patrol at the Davenport Towers. I was introduced to Curtis and advised him that I had been assigned to investigate this incident. Curtis stated he only wanted his wallet back and wanted to keep the incident as low key as possible. He did not want to pursue charges.

Curtis stated that on 10/26/07 at approximately 0100 hours he drove to the Hollywood Erotic Boutique at 9611 E. Sprague. While he was there, a white male with short brown hair, about 5'10 to 6', slender with possible stubble on his face, in his mid to late 20's, bummed a cigarette from Curtis. He asked Curtis if Curtis was a cop and asked if he wanted to get together. Curtis said he told the male he would not pay for sex because that would be prostitution. He told the male he would give the male $100 to "help him out for gas." He also gave the male some cigarettes. He told the male he didn't care if they got together and had sex or not. Curtis ultimately gave the male his cell phone number of ███████ ██████ and told the male to call him if he wanted to get together later. Curtis did not give the male any money at that time.

Curtis stated while he was in the Hollywood Erotic Boutique, he talked to the female employee. She gave him her name, Jalene, and phone number of 443-

2
SPOKANE POLICE DEPARTMENT
ADDITIONAL REPORT

DATE/TIME: 10/27/07   CASE NO.:   07-808376

CHARGE/INCIDENT: EXTORTION

FURTHER INVESTIGATION   DET. TIM MADSEN 366

4805. Curtis stated that the female could confirm he offered to give the male $100 to help him out and there should be video inside the Hollywood Erotic Boutique verifying his contact with the suspect and it may include their conversation.

Curtis stated he left the Hollywood Erotic Boutique in his white Honda and drove to Northern Quest Casino. At about 0300 hours he received a call on his cell phone from the male he had met at the Hollywood Erotic Boutique. The male asked him if he wanted to get together and they agreed to meet at the Davenport Towers Hotel. Curtis drove to the Davenport Towers where he met the male after he saw the male walk away from a blue sedan which was parked outside the hotel. The male was alone.   Curtis did not recall what clothing the male was wearing and never knew his name.

Curtis stated both he and the male walked into the lobby together. He told the male again that he would give the male $100 to help him out but he was not paying him to have sex. Curtis and the male went up to Curtis' room, which was 968. Once in the room, Curtis gave the male $100. While they were in the room, they both had a bottle of Propel fitness water.   Curtis and the male ultimately had anal intercourse on the bed in Curtis' hotel room. The male performed intercourse on Curtis and the male's semen and/or DNA would be on the inside of the condom while Curtis' DNA would be on the exterior. Curtis stated he was the person who received the anal sex.

Curtis stated he went to sleep with the male. Curtis woke up alone a little before 0700 hours and he received a phone call from the male. The male told Curtis he had Curtis' wallet and knew he was a state legislator and married. The male claimed to have taken explicit photos of Curtis while Curtis was asleep. The male threatened to publicly release this information unless Curtis gave the male $1,000.   Curtis looked for his billfold and discovered it had been taken from his jacket.   Curtis kept his money separate from his billfold. Inside his billfold however was his driver's license, business ID and a Bank One credit card in Curtis' name. He described his billfold as a bi-fold style, black in color with a yellow interior.

Curtis stated he agreed to give the male an additional $200 in an envelope, if he got his wallet back. Curtis stated he went to the front desk and got a Davenport Hotel envelope from the hotel staff. Curtis waited in the lobby and ultimately gave the envelope containing $200 to hotel registration staff with a name the male told him to write on the envelope. He didn't remember the name. A second

3
SPOKANE POLICE DEPARTMENT
ADDITIONAL REPORT

DATE/TIME: 10/27/07   CASE NO.:   07-808376

CHARGE/INCIDENT: EXTORTION

FURTHER INVESTIGATION   DET. TIM MADSEN 366

white male picked up the envelope. He described the second white male as having short brown hair, about the same size as the first white male with a scruffy mustache. The second white male took the envelope and walked out of the lobby. He got into the same blue sedan he had seen the first male in the previous evening. As the vehicle drove away, Curtis wrote down the license number, Washington license ▓▓▓▓▓▓▓

Curtis stated he talked to a friend in the Washington State Patrol. Curtis said he wanted the Washington State Patrol to investigate the incident because the local police would talk and it would get out to the press.

I told Curtis that I wanted to collect evidence in this case so that it could be secured in case it was ever needed in the future. If he wished no further action taken, I would still have any critical evidence in case he changed his mind or the suspect continued to threaten Curtis in the future. I told Curtis that the toothpaste was already out of the tube. Curtis told me he was just trying to "put the cap back on the tube." I told Curtis that the suspect may victimize other people in the future and Curtis acknowledged that part of his job was to protect people in the State of Washington. Lt. McGovern told Curtis no matter what happened, we would have to document the case in report form regardless of whether or not the case was prosecuted. Curtis said he wished he would have just paid the additional money to the suspect because he didn't wish the case to be prosecuted. If the incident became public it could cost him his marriage and career.

While Lt. McGovern, Sgt. Wade and I were talking to Curtis, Curtis received a call on his cell phone at 1139 hours. Curtis tipped the phone so that I could hear the conversation. I heard a male voice telling Curtis he was on his way back into town and that he wanted Curtis to leave $800 in the last flower pot on the west side Washington St. Bridge at the far north end. He stated he would be there in 25 minutes to pick up the money. Curtis asked the male how he would get his billfold back. The male told Curtis that he would drop it off at the front desk of the hotel lobby after he received the money. Curtis said all the incoming calls from the suspect on his Blackberry showed as restricted numbers.

Lt. McGovern contacted SIU personnel to conduct surveillance on the specific flower pot on the Washington St. Bridge. Surveillance personnel were also supplied with Washington license number ▓▓▓▓▓▓ which returned to a ▓▓▓▓
▓▓▓

4
SPOKANE POLICE DEPARTMENT
ADDITIONAL REPORT

DATE/TIME: 10/27/07   CASE NO.:   07-808376

CHARGE/INCIDENT: EXTORTION

FURTHER INVESTIGATION   DET. TIM MADSEN 366

At 1212 hours a male called Curtis' cell phone number again, telling Curtis he should have had plenty of time to get the money. I directed Curtis to stall the male, giving surveillance units time to set up. I heard the male tell Curtis that he was going to have a friend pick up the money. After he received his money the billfold would be dropped off at the hotel. Curtis said the incoming phone calls showed restricted.

At 1237 hours Lt. McGovern advised me that surveillance personnel were set up and ready for the victim to drop an envelope off on the bridge. I followed Curtis to his vehicle and told him to drive directly to the north end of the bridge where he would be under surveillance. I told Curtis to drop the envelope off, return to his car and drive directly back to the hotel.

At 1242 hours Curtis called me on my cell phone. He told me that he saw the first white male walking south bound on the north end of the Washington St. Bridge toward the park. He said the male was wearing a white colored baseball shirt but he could not describe the clothing further. I immediately phoned Lt. McGovern so he could advise surveillance personnel. Lt. McGovern also advised me that Curtis had already dropped off the envelope and was driving back south bound in his white Honda.

I called Curtis back and he confirmed he had already dropped off the envelope and he last saw the male walking through the park. I told Curtis to immediately drive back to his hotel.

Once Curtis returned to the hotel, we went back to room 968 and I continued to interview him. I read a search consent card to him, which he stated he understood and signed. Curtis did supply me with a buccal swab/DNA sample in case it was needed at a later date. Curtis used a buccal swab applicator to swab the inside of his cheeks, allowing me to collect two samples.

I asked Curtis what physical evidence would be in the hotel room which would link the suspect to the hotel room. Curtis pointed out a Propel fitness water bottle in the garbage, a condom wrapper in the garbage and a used condom in the garbage. I photographed the room and the items prior to their collection. I also collected the sheets and pillow cases from the bed.

While I was collecting evidence I saw a plastic sack which contained a light grey length of nylon rope, a plastic doctor's stethoscope and other items I could not

5
SPOKANE POLICE DEPARTMENT
ADDITIONAL REPORT

DATE/TIME: 10/27/07   CASE NO.: 07-808376

CHARGE/INCIDENT: EXTORTION

FURTHER INVESTIGATION   DET. TIM MADSEN 366

immediately identify. Curtis told me they had nothing to do with the sex act and the suspect had not handled them. Curtis said he did not want to show me those items in the sack. I did not view the items further because Curtis said they had nothing to do with the case.

The pillow cases, sheets, Propel bottle, condom and condom wrapper were ultimately placed onto the property book as evidence.

I contacted hotel security officer John Clarke. I told Clarke that I had collected the sheets and pillow cases from #968 as evidence and the occupant of the room was the reported victim of a crime.

I was contacted by Lt. McGovern, who advised me that surveillance personnel had detained a white male who had picked the envelope up on the north end of the Washington St. Bridge. I drove Curtis to the north end of the bridge in my vehicle for a show up. I told him the person detained may or may not be involved in the incident. I asked him if he recognized that person as anyone he had seen reference this incident. Curtis looked at the male, who was later identified as Brandon Burchell. Curtis stated he had never seen the male before. I transported Curtis back to the hotel and returned to the Public Safety Building to question Burchell.

I arrived at the Public Safety Building where Brandon Dean Burchell was ▓▓▓▓▓ in an interview room in the Major Crimes Unit. ▓▓▓▓▓ I told him that I was investigating an extortion complaint and that I wanted to talk to him and get his side of the story. ▓▓▓▓▓. I told him he did not have to talk to me if he didn't want to, he could pick and choose what he wanted to say and he could stop talking to me at any point in time. I asked him if he had ever ▓▓▓▓▓▓▓▓▓▓▓ and Burchell said he had. ▓▓▓▓▓

Burchell said his name was Brandon Dean Burchell, ▓▓/83, and he lived at ▓▓▓ ▓▓▓▓▓ His personal cell number is ▓▓▓▓▓ The service carrier is TMobile.

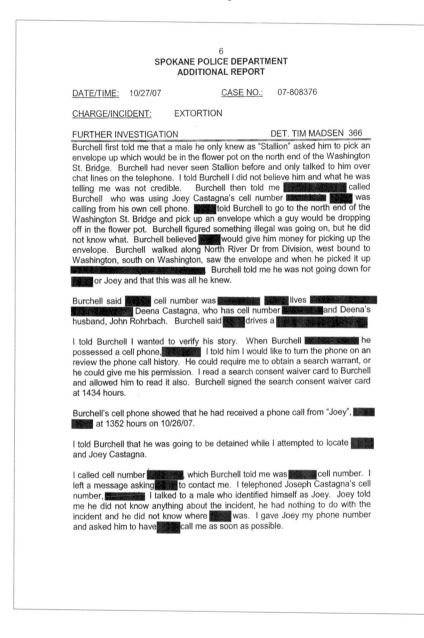

6
SPOKANE POLICE DEPARTMENT
ADDITIONAL REPORT

DATE/TIME: 10/27/07   CASE NO.:   07-808376

CHARGE/INCIDENT: EXTORTION

FURTHER INVESTIGATION   DET. TIM MADSEN 366

Burchell first told me that a male he only knew as "Stallion" asked him to pick an envelope up which would be in the flower pot on the north end of the Washington St. Bridge. Burchell had never seen Stallion before and only talked to him over chat lines on the telephone. I told Burchell I did not believe him and what he was telling me was not credible. Burchell then told me ███████████ called Burchell who was using Joey Castagna's cell number ████████ ████ was calling from his own cell phone. ████ told Burchell to go to the north end of the Washington St. Bridge and pick up an envelope which a guy would be dropping off in the flower pot. Burchell figured something illegal was going on, but he did not know what. Burchell believed ████ would give him money for picking up the envelope. Burchell walked along North River Dr from Division, west bound to Washington, south on Washington, saw the envelope and when he picked it up ████████████████████. Burchell told me he was not going down for ██ or Joey and that this was all he knew.

Burchell said ████ cell number was ████████ ████ lives ██████████ ██████████ Deena Castagna, who has cell number ████████ and Deena's husband, John Rohrbach. Burchell said ██ drives a ████████████

I told Burchell I wanted to verify his story. When Burchell ██████████ he possessed a cell phone, ████████ I told him I would like to turn the phone on an review the phone call history. He could require me to obtain a search warrant, or he could give me his permission. I read a search consent waiver card to Burchell and allowed him to read it also. Burchell signed the search consent waiver card at 1434 hours.

Burchell's cell phone showed that he had received a phone call from "Joey", ████ ████ at 1352 hours on 10/26/07.

I told Burchell that he was going to be detained while I attempted to locate ████ and Joey Castagna.

I called cell number ████████, which Burchell told me was ████ cell number. I left a message asking ████ to contact me. I telephoned Joseph Castagna's cell number, ████████ I talked to a male who identified himself as Joey. Joey told me he did not know anything about the incident, he had nothing to do with the incident and he did not know where ████ was. I gave Joey my phone number and asked him to have ████ call me as soon as possible.

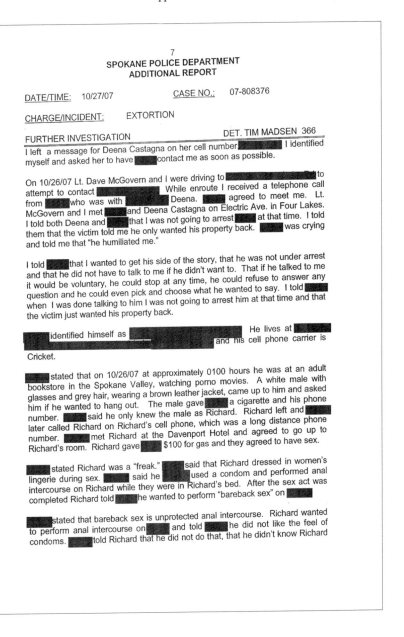

7

SPOKANE POLICE DEPARTMENT
ADDITIONAL REPORT

DATE/TIME: 10/27/07   CASE NO.:   07-808376

CHARGE/INCIDENT: EXTORTION

FURTHER INVESTIGATION   DET. TIM MADSEN 366

I left a message for Deena Castagna on her cell number ▮▮▮▮▮▮ I identified myself and asked her to have ▮▮▮ contact me as soon as possible.

On 10/26/07 Lt. Dave McGovern and I were driving to ▮▮▮▮▮▮▮▮▮▮▮▮ to attempt to contact ▮▮▮▮▮▮ While enroute I received a telephone call from ▮▮▮▮ who was with ▮▮▮▮ Deena. ▮▮▮▮ agreed to meet me. Lt. McGovern and I met ▮▮▮ and Deena Castagna on Electric Ave. in Four Lakes. I told both Deena and ▮▮▮ that I was not going to arrest ▮▮▮ at that time. I told them that the victim told me he only wanted his property back. ▮▮▮▮ was crying and told me that "he humiliated me."

I told ▮▮▮ that I wanted to get his side of the story, that he was not under arrest and that he did not have to talk to me if he didn't want to. That if he talked to me it would be voluntary, he could stop at any time, he could refuse to answer any question and he could even pick and choose what he wanted to say. I told ▮▮▮▮ when I was done talking to him I was not going to arrest him at that time and that the victim just wanted his property back.

▮▮▮▮▮▮ identified himself as ▮▮▮▮▮▮▮▮ He lives at ▮▮▮▮▮ ▮▮▮▮▮▮▮▮▮▮▮▮ and his cell phone carrier is Cricket.

▮▮▮▮ stated that on 10/26/07 at approximately 0100 hours he was at an adult bookstore in the Spokane Valley, watching porno movies. A white male with glasses and grey hair, wearing a brown leather jacket, came up to him and asked him if he wanted to hang out. The male gave ▮▮▮▮ a cigarette and his phone number. ▮▮▮▮ said he only knew the male as Richard. Richard left and ▮▮▮▮ later called Richard on Richard's cell phone, which was a long distance phone number. ▮▮▮▮ met Richard at the Davenport Hotel and agreed to go up to Richard's room. Richard gave ▮▮▮▮ $100 for gas and they agreed to have sex.

▮▮▮▮ stated Richard was a "freak." ▮▮▮▮ said that Richard dressed in women's lingerie during sex. ▮▮▮▮ said he ▮▮▮▮ used a condom and performed anal intercourse on Richard while they were in Richard's bed. After the sex act was completed Richard told ▮▮▮ he wanted to perform "bareback sex" on ▮▮▮▮

▮▮▮▮ stated that bareback sex is unprotected anal intercourse. Richard wanted to perform anal intercourse on ▮▮▮▮ and told ▮▮▮▮ he did not like the feel of condoms. ▮▮▮▮ told Richard that he did not do that, that he didn't know Richard

8
SPOKANE POLICE DEPARTMENT
ADDITIONAL REPORT

DATE/TIME: 10/27/07   CASE NO.:   07-808376

CHARGE/INCIDENT: EXTORTION

FURTHER INVESTIGATION   DET. TIM MADSEN 366

and that "bareback sex" was unsafe sex and was dangerous. Richard asked
█████ "what would it take for you to do it."

Richard asked █████ if he would let Richard perform bareback sex on █████ for
$1,000. █████ agreed and Richard performed unprotected anal sex on █████
Richard fell asleep after the intercourse. █████ woke Richard up and asked him
about the money Richard promised █████ Richard stated he did not have any
more money and could not get it at that hour. █████ asked Richard for collateral
and Richard gave █████ his billfold to hold until he received the rest of his money.
█████ left the Davenport with the billfold.

█████ said he called Richard at about 0645 hours and asked for the rest of his
money.   Richard said he didn't have any more money to give him. █████
admitted he had called Richard and told him to put the rest of the money in an
envelope and leave it on the bridge. █████ would give Richard his billfold back
after █████ got the rest of his money.

█████ said after he found out that Brandon Burchell █████████████████ he
gave Richard's billfold to a black male known to him only as Kalani (unknown
spelling.) █████ stated Kalani had been at ██████████████ This is the
residence of █████████ Mike Castagna. The billfold was placed in a purple
and peach colored gift bag. He gave it to Kalani to get rid of. █████ admitted he
had looked through the billfold and saw that Richard had identification which said
he was a member of Congress or something.

█████ continually cried and said that he believed Richard had tricked him and
never intended to pay him the thousand dollars for unprotected sex.

█████ told me Kalani had called █████ and told █████ that the billfold was hidden in
a dumpster at Augusta/Wall.

█████ told me Richard's driver's license was left at the Holiday Gas Station on
395, north of the North Division Y. He had told Richard he left the ID with the
employees so that Richard would have his ID to get money out of the bank.

I told █████ that I would like to have ████████████ I told him he could
require that I obtain a search warrant prior to ██████████████ told
me he would willingly ██████████████ I read a search consent waiver card to
█████████████████ and allowed him to read it as well.

9

SPOKANE POLICE DEPARTMENT
ADDITIONAL REPORT

DATE/TIME: 10/27/07   CASE NO.: 07-808376

CHARGE/INCIDENT: EXTORTION

FURTHER INVESTIGATION   DET. TIM MADSEN 366

I gave ▮▮▮ my business card and told him he was free to go. ▮▮▮▮▮▮
▮▮▮▮▮▮ placed onto property as evidence.

Lt. McGovern and I drove to Augusta/Wall. The apartment complex located on
the north east corner is ▮▮▮▮▮▮▮▮▮▮ Behind the complex was a green
dumpster. I located a purple/peach colored gift bag in the bottom of the
dumpster. Inside the gift bag was a leather wallet with credit cards and
identification belonging to Richard Curtis. The gift bag and billfold with contents
were placed onto property as evidence.

Lt. McGovern advised me that he had driven to the Holiday station and had
recovered Curtis' driver's license from station employees. See. Lt. McGovern's
report for details. Det. Mark Burbridge contacted station employee Donna
Foster, see Det. Burbridge's report for further details.

FURTHER INVESTIGATION

DETECTIVE TIM MADSEN 366

Major Crimes Unit
10/27/07 sc

APPENDIX D

Professor Anita F. Hill
Senate Judiciary Committee
October 11, 1991

Mr. Chairman, Senator Thurmond, Members of the Committee, my name is Anita P. Hill, and I am a Professor of Law at the University of Oklahoma. I was born on a farm in Okmulge, Oklahoma in 1956, the 13th child, and had my early education there. My father is Albert Hill, a farmer of that area. My mother's name is Erma Hill, she is also a farmer and housewife. My childhood was the childhood of both work and poverty; but it was one of solid family affection as represented by my parents religious atmosphere in the Baptist faith and I have been a member of the Antioch Baptist Church in Tulsa since 1983. It remains a warm part of my life at the present time.

For my undergraduate work I went to Oklahoma State University and graduated in 1977. I am attaching to this statement my resume with further details of my education. I graduated from the university with academic honors and proceeded to the Yale Law School where I received my J.D. degree in 1980.

Upon graduation from law school I became a practicing lawyer with the Washington, D.C. firm of Wald, Harkrader & Ross. In 1981, I was introduced to now Judge Thomas by a mutual friend. Judge Thomas told me that he anticipated a political appointment shortly and asked if I might be interested in working in that office. He was in fact appointed as Assistant Secretary of Education, in which capacity he was the Director of the Office for Civil Rights. After he was in that post, he asked if I would become his assistant and I did then accept that position. In my early period, there I had two major projects. The first was an article I wrote for Judge Thomas' signature on Education of Minority Students. The second was the organization of a seminar on high risk students, which was abandoned because

Judge Thomas transferred to the EEOC before that project was completed.

During this period at the Department of Education, my working relationship with Judge Thomas was positive. I had a good deal of responsibility as well as independence. I thought that he respected my work and that he trusted my judgment. After approximately three months of working together, he asked me to go out with him socially. I declined and explained to him that I thought that it would only jeopardize what, at the time, I considered to be a very good working relationship. I had a normal social life with other men outside of the office and, I believed then, as now, that having a social relationship with a person who was supervising my work would be ill-advised. I was very uncomfortable with the idea and told him so.

I thought that by saying "no" and explaining my reasons, my employer would abandon his social suggestions. However, to my regret, in the following few weeks he continued to ask me out on several occasions. He pressed me to justify my reasons for saying "no" to him. These incidents took place in his office or mine. They were in the form of private conversations which would not have been overheard by anyone else.

My working relationship became even more strained when Judge Thomas began to use work situations to discuss sex. On these occasions he would call me into his office for reports on education issues and projects or he might suggest that because of time pressures we go to lunch at a government cafeteria. After a brief discussion of work he would turn the conversation to discussion of sexual matters. His conversations were very vivid.

He spoke about acts that he had seen in pornographic films involving such matters as women having sex with animals and films showing group sex or rape scenes. He talked about pornographic materials depicting individuals with large penises or large breasts involved in various sex acts. On several occasions Thomas told me graphically of his own sexual prowess.

Because I was extremely uncomfortable talking about sex with him at all and particularly in such a graphic way, I told him that I did not want to talk about those subjects. I would also try to change the subject to education matters or to nonsexual personal matters such as his background or beliefs. My efforts to change the subject were rarely successful.

Throughout the period of these conversations, he also from time-to-time asked me for social engagements. My reactions to these conversations was to avoid having them by eliminating opportunities for us to engage in extended conversations. This was difficult because I was his only assistant at the Office for Civil Rights. During the latter part of my time at the Department of Education, the social pressures and any conversations of this offensive kind ended. I began both to believe and hope that our working relationship could be on a proper, cordial and professional base.

When Judge Thomas was made Chairman of the EEOC, I needed to face the question of whether to go with him. I was asked to do so. I did. The work itself was interesting and at that time it appeared that the sexual overtures which had so troubled me had ended. I also faced the realistic fact that I had no alternative job. While I might have gone back to private practice, perhaps in my old firm or at another, I was dedicated he in that field. Moreover, the Department of Education itself was a dubious venture; President Reagan was seeking to abolish the entire Department at that time.

For my first months at the EEOC, where I continued as an assistant to Judge Thomas, there were no sexual conversations or overtures. However, during the Fall and Winter of 1982, these began again. The comments were random and ranged from pressing me about why I didn't go out with him to remarks about my personal appearance. I remember his saying that someday I would have to give him the real reason that I wouldn't go out with him. He began to show real displeasure in his tone of voice, his demeanor and his continued pressure for an explanation. He commented on what I was wearing in terms of whether it made me more or less sexually attractive. The incidents occurred in his inner office at the EEOC.

One of the oddest episodes I remember was an occasion in which Thomas was drinking a Coke in his office. He got up from the table at which we were working, went over to his desk to get the Coke, looked at the can, and said, "Who has put pubic hair on my Coke?" On other occasions he referred to the size of his own penis as being larger than normal and he also spoke on some occasions of the pleasures he had given to women with oral sex.

At this point, late 1982, 1 began to feel severe stress on the job. I began to be concerned that Clarence Thomas might take it out on me by downgrading me or not giving me important assignments. I also thought that he might find an excuse for dismissing me.

In January of 1983, I began looking for another job. I was handicapped because I feared that if he found out, he might make it difficult for me to find to her employment and I might be dismissed from the job I had. Another factor that made my search more difficult was that this was a period of a government hiring freeze. In February, 1983, 1 was hospitalized for five days on an emergency basis for an acute stomach pain which I attributed to stress on the job. Once out of the hospital, I became more committed to find other employment and sought further to minimize my contact with Thomas. This became easier when Allyson Duncan became office director because most of my work was handled with her and I had contact with Clarence Thomas mostly in staff meetings.

In the Spring of 1983, an opportunity to teach law at Oral Roberts University opened up. I agreed to take the job In large part because of my desire to escape the pressures I felt at the EEOC due to Thomas. When I informed him that I was leaving in July, I recall that his response was that now I "would no longer have an excuse for not going out with" him. I told him that I still preferred not to do so.

At some time after that meeting, he asked if he could take me to dinner at the end of my term. When I declined, he assured me that the dinner was a professional courtesy only and not a social invitation. I reluctantly agreed to accept that invitation but only if it was at the very end of a workday. On, as I recall, the last day of my employment at the EEOC in the summer of 1983, I did have dinner with Clarence Thomas. We went directly from work to a restaurant near the office. We talked about the work I had done both at Education and at EEOC. He told me that he was pleased with all of it except for an article and speech that I done for him when we were at the Office for Civil Rights. Finally, he made a comment which I vividly remember. He said that if I ever told anyone about his behavior toward me it could ruin his career. This was not an apology nor was there any explanation. That was his last remark about the possibility of our going out or reference to his behavior.

In July 1983, I left the Washington, D.C. area and have had minimal contact with Judge Clarence Thomas since.

I am of course aware from the press that some question has been raised about conversations I had with Judge Clarence Thomas after I left the EEOC. From 1983 until today I have seen Judge Clarence Thomas only twice. On one occasion I needed to get a reference from him and on another he made a public appearance In Tulsa. On one occasion he called me at home and we had an inconsequential conversation. On one other occasion he called me without reaching me and I returned the call without reaching him and nothing came of it. I have, on at least three occasions been asked to act as a conduit for others.

I knew his secretary, Diane Holt, well when I was with the EEOC. There were occasions on which I spoke to her and on some of those occasions undoubtedly I passed on some casual comment to Thomas.

There was a series of calls in the first three months of 1985 occasioned by a group in Tulsa which wished to have a civil rights conference; they wanted Thomas to be the speaker, and enlisted my assistance for this purpose. I did call in January and February to no effect and finally suggested to the person directly involved, Susan Cahall, that she put the matter back into her own hands and call directly. She did do that in March of 1985.

In connection with that March invitation to Tulsa by Ms. Cahall, which was for a seminar conference some research was needed; I was asked to try to get the research work and did attempt to do so by a call to Thomas. There was another call about another possible conference in July of 1985.

In August of 1987, I was in Washington and I did call Diane Holt. In the course of this conversation she asked me how long I was going to be in town and I told her; she recorded it as August 15; it was in fact August 20. She told me about Thomas' marriage and I did say "congratulate him."

It is only after a great deal of agonizing consideration that I am able to talk of these unpleasant matter to anyone, except my closest friends. Telling the world is the most difficult experience of my life. I was aware that he could effect my future career did not wish to burn all my bridges. I may have used poor judgment; perhaps I should have taken angry or even militant steps, both when I was in the agency or after I had left it, but I must confess to the world that the course I took seemed the better, as well as the easier approach. I declined any comment to newspapers, but later, when Senate staff asked me about these matters, I felt that I had a duty to report. I have no personal vendetta against Clarence Thomas. I seek only to provide the Committee with information which it may regard as relevant. It would have been more comfortable to remain silent. I took no initiative to inform anyone. But when I was asked by a representative of this committee to report my experience, I felt that I had to tell the truth.

The CHAIRMAN. *Thank you.*

INDEX

Win McCormack | **YOU DON'T KNOW ME**

First and foremost, I need to thank Lee Montgomery, editorial director of Tin House Books, without whose unwavering determination and encouragement this project would not have even begun; Carol Butler, who introduced me to Mike Rice, my stalwart guide on this sometimes very amusing but more often horrifying journey through the depths of the Republican underworld, and who also provided intellectual and emotional support throughout; and Tony D. Perez of the Tin House Books staff, almost a coauthor, whose yeoman work on every aspect of the main text was also a sine qua non.

This book was indeed, even more than most, a collective effort. In addition to my debt to Tony, I owe debts of gratitude to Tin House Books intern Noor ("The Queen") Hashem for her intrepid and resourceful research for the introduction, and especially for saving me from one particularly embarrassing mistake; former *Tin House* magazine staff editor Ben George for his meticulous fact-checking; Tin House Books editor Meg Storey for her painstaking copy editing and production oversight; and Tin House Books publicity director Deborah Jayne for her wildly successful (here's hoping anyway!) promotion efforts. Finally, I need to express my gratitude to designer Laura Shaw, who applied both her great creative skill and innumerable hours of labor to this unruly and potentially off-putting material, with such fine results.

As always when I attempt to theorize seriously about politics, I realize how great my intellectual debt remains to my original mentors in political analysis at Harvard, most especially Martin Peretz and Samuel P. Huntington (though I don't know if either of those two eminences would fully endorse this particular project).

Mike Rice oversaw the exhaustive empirical research at VR Associates. Michael Simon and Dan Barr supervised the equally rigorous libel review within the Perkins, Coie law firm.

—WLM